INSTANT POSITIVITY

365 Ways to Become
1% Better Every Day

KRISTEN BUTLER

POWER OF POSITIVITY

ALSO BY KRISTEN BUTLER

3 Minute Positivity Journal: Boost Your Mood. Train Your Mind. Change Your Life.

3 Minute Happiness Journal: Create Happy Habits. Change Your Brain. Transform Your Life.

The Comfort Zone: Create a Life You Really Love with Less Stress and More Flow

The Key to Positivity: Why You've Got the Comfort Zone All Wrong–and How to Tap Its Power to Live Your Best Life

Paperback ISBN: 978-1-7379704-8-4
ePUB ISBN: 978-1-7379704-9-1

Library of Congress Control Number: 2024925010

Interior Design: Olivier Darbonville
Cover Design: Ishtiaq Ahmad
Cover Photography: Shutterstock, Stock Photo ID: 711317101
Author Headshot Photography: Michael & Anna Costa Photography

Published by Power of Positivity, LLC
Asheville, North Carolina
www.powerofpositivity.com

Printed in the United States of America

Introduction

Welcome, friend! You're holding more than a book—this is your daily guide to a happier, more fulfilled *you*.

From my rock-bottom journey to discovering my true passion and joy, I've learned that positivity is a commitment—a choice you make every day. This book is your guide to making that choice a little easier.

Positivity isn't just a mood—it's a lifestyle. It's the small steps, the 1% improvements, and the simple acts of kindness you give to yourself and others. Together, we'll make positivity a habit. As you build that habit, you'll see it ripple into every part of your life.

Positivity starts with daily choices that align with who you want to become. Each entry in this book is designed to be a spark—an action, an affirmation, a slight shift in perspective to light up your day. These small changes bring significant results over time, and each one supports you in living with purpose, peace, and positivity.

This book is the companion you didn't realize was missing from your life. My mission is to help you create real, lasting change—a change that doesn't come from giant leaps; it comes from small, consistent action steps.

Why Positivity Matters

Imagine adding a dose of positivity to each day. Little by little, these moments build a life you love: healthier habits, more meaningful relationships, work that energizes you, and, most importantly, a deep appreciation for who you are and the life you're creating. When you show up for yourself daily, everything changes.

What to Expect from This Book

This book is your companion for a year of positive change—1% at a time. Real growth doesn't happen overnight; it happens over time. Each day's entry stands on its own, but together, they guide you toward becoming your best self.

Throughout this journey, you'll explore twelve core pillars of positivity: *Gratitude, Service, Wellness, Balance, Presence, Joy, Purpose, Success, Resilience, Faith, Authenticity,* and *Abundance.* Each pillar is spread throughout the year, allowing you to connect deeply and grow stronger in each area. These principles have transformed my life and the lives of millions in our community.

How to Use Each Entry

Each day, you'll find a quote, reflection, and action step designed to make positivity practical. Here's how to make the most of each entry:

- **Read the Quote**: Begin with the day's quote as an anchor for reflection.
- **Engage with the Reflection**: These short, impactful thoughts help you connect deeply with the theme. Take a moment to let the message resonate with you.

- **Take Action:** This is where positivity becomes real. Each step is simple but meaningful, releasing happy "feel-good" chemicals—dopamine, serotonin, and oxytocin. As you follow through, you nurture your mind, body, and spirit and those around you.

- **Affirmation**: Close each entry by saying the day's affirmation aloud. Let it be your reminder, intention, and mindset for the day. As a bonus, recite the affirmation in front of the mirror, looking into your eyes. This practice is called mirror work.

Start anywhere, any day. Remember, you're choosing to grow 1% daily—these small, ordinary moments add to extraordinary transformation.

Make It Your Own

Consider keeping a notebook or journal nearby. Each morning, reflect on how you'll incorporate the day's lesson and, in the evening, note any positive shifts or insights. If journaling isn't your thing, commit to taking each action. Small steps lead to big changes.

This Book is Your "Positivity Feed"

Let this book be your antidote to "doom-scrolling." Set aside a moment each day to invest in yourself. Filling up on positivity instead of instant gratification will shift your mood, elevate your spirit, and brighten your mindset. These daily moments build momentum, inviting more of what you want into your life.

Your Journey Begins Now

By choosing this journey, you're investing in your happiness and future. Each day you read this book, you unlock more of your potential.

I'm so excited to start this journey with you! Let's stay connected—I'd love to hear about your transformations over the year.

Here's to your growth, one day and one positive step at a time.

Cheering for you,

Kristen

P.S. Let's connect! Scan the QR code
or text "INSTANT" to 828-237-6082*
*US and Canada only.

January

START WITH GRATITUDE

"Gratitude turns what we have into enough. It makes sense of our past, brings peace for today, and creates a vision for tomorrow."

– MELODY BEATTIE

Gratitude can transform your life. Starting your day with gratitude sets a positive tone and improves your well-being. Research shows daily gratitude boosts happiness, reduces stress, and enhances emotional resilience. Have you tried it consistently? In the Power of Positivity community, we've seen how focusing on gratitude shifts perspectives, turning challenges into opportunities. Remember: embracing gratitude doesn't mean ignoring difficulties. It means you acknowledge what's good and lean into moments of peace and positivity.

TODAY'S ACTION

Write down three things you're grateful for, and take a few minutes to immerse yourself in the *feeling* of appreciation. Be specific about why these aspects matter to you. This practice deepens your sense of gratitude and anchors you in the present, setting you up with a mindset of abundance.

TODAY'S AFFIRMATION

I am grateful today and every day.

JAN
FEB
MAR
APR
MAY
JUN
JUL
AUG
SEP
OCT
NOV
DEC

January 2

TRANSFORM WITH POSITIVITY

"Change your thoughts, and you change your world."

—NORMAN VINCENT PEALE

Positivity starts within. Your thoughts shape how you see the world, sending out a ripple that impacts everything around you. Choosing positive and empowering thoughts invites more peace, joy, and purpose. This simple shift transforms your mindset and environment, attracting people, opportunities, and experiences that reflect your light.

TODAY'S ACTION

Start a "Positivity Ripple" by uplifting those around you. Compliment a friend, express gratitude to a coworker, or do a random act of kindness. Notice how these small, positive actions shift the energy in your environment. Each interaction reflects the positivity you're cultivating within, creating a ripple of joy and connection that enhances everyone's day—including yours.

TODAY'S AFFIRMATION

I create a positive world by choosing thoughts and actions that uplift and inspire.

BELIEVE IN YOUR POWER

"Whether you think you can, or you think you can't—you're right."

—Henry Ford

Positivity begins with belief. When you believe in yourself, you open doors to endless possibilities. Every day, you have the choice to approach life with confidence, embracing challenges as opportunities for growth. This belief creates resilience, fueling your ability to push forward no matter what comes your way. Positivity is a powerful tool that changes how you experience life.

TODAY'S ACTION

Today, take one small step that reflects a belief in your potential. Choose something meaningful to you—a goal, a dream, or a simple action that aligns with your best self. Then, act on it, knowing that this is a choice to strengthen your self-belief. Notice how this decision fuels your positivity and sets the tone for the day ahead.

TODAY'S AFFIRMATION

I believe in my power to create a positive life.

INSTANT POSITIVITY   **15**

JAN
FEB
MAR
APR
MAY
JUN
JUL
AUG
SEP
OCT
NOV
DEC

January 4

WALKING FOR WELLNESS

"An early-morning walk is a blessing for the whole day."

—Henry David Thoreau

A walk is more than just movement; it's a reset for the mind, body, and spirit. Each step releases tension, lifts your mood, and connects you to the present moment. Walking is one of the simplest yet most transformative forms of self-care. Whether strolling through nature or taking a path around your neighborhood, walking gives you space to unwind, reflect, and soak in the beauty around you. It's a powerful reminder that sometimes the best things in life are free.

TODAY'S ACTION

Make time for a 20-minute walk today, ideally in a green space like a park or trail. As you walk, focus on your breath and observe the sights and sounds around you. Notice the colors of the leaves, the sun's warmth, or the air's crispness. Please leave your phone behind or put it on silent to fully immerse yourself. Feel the stress melt away, and let your steps ground you in the present.

TODAY'S AFFIRMATION

With each step, I find clarity, peace, and gratitude.

STEP INTO YOUR PURPOSE

"The two most important days in your life are the day
you are born and the day you find out why."

—MARK TWAIN

Finding your purpose is like unlocking a hidden power within you. It gives each day a more profound meaning and fills even the smallest moments with joy and intention. When you align your actions with what matters, life flows with resilience, gratitude, and positivity. Purpose transforms ordinary days into stepping stones toward something extraordinary.

TODAY'S ACTION

Take a moment to reflect on what fills you with energy and makes you feel alive. Write down one thing that connects you to something greater. Now, find a small way to weave this purpose into your day—reaching out to a loved one, dedicating a few minutes to a passion project, or sharing kindness. Let this action be a powerful reminder of your unique path.

TODAY'S AFFIRMATION

I embrace my purpose with joy and clarity.

HYDRATE FOR HAPPINESS

"Your body's natural state is one of health. Give it the right tools—starting with water—and watch it thrive."

—Dr. Mark Hyman

Water is life's simplest yet most potent fuel. Our bodies are incredible, designed to function at their best when adequately hydrated. Yet, in times of stress or busyness, we overlook our most basic need: water. Every cell, organ, and system depends on water to perform, heal, and energize. Hydration does more than quench thirst—it supports clearer thinking, balances mood, boosts energy and helps you feel vibrant. Just a few mindful sips can be a game-changer for your body and mind.

TODAY'S ACTION

Start your morning with a tall glass of water, setting the tone for a hydrated day. Keep a water bottle handy, and set a fun hourly goal to stay on track. Add lemon, cucumber, or a pinch of sea salt for a refreshing twist, and notice how each sip fuels clarity, energy, and calm. By the end of the day, celebrate how this small habit boosts your mood, focus, and vitality.

TODAY'S AFFIRMATION

I honor my body with water and feel vibrant and alive.

JUST GET STARTED

"You don't have to get it perfect; you just have to get it going."

—AMY PORTERFIELD

Perfection can paralyze your dreams. Waiting for everything to be "just right" keeps you stuck in place, holding back your potential. Actual progress is built on taking action rather than on achieving perfection. Each small, imperfect step moves you closer to your goals and builds confidence. Success favors those who begin, even when the path could be clearer.

TODAY'S ACTION

Choose one project, goal, or idea you've been holding back on, waiting for the "right time." Take one small step to move it forward—send that email, sketch your plan, create that content, or schedule a time to start. Commit to imperfect action today. Focus on building momentum, not achieving perfection.

TODAY'S AFFIRMATION

I choose progress over perfection, trusting each step brings me closer to my goals.

January 8

LIFT YOUR COMMUNITY

"We rise by lifting others."

—Robert Ingersoll

When we lift others, we elevate ourselves. Every act of support, big or small, creates a ripple of kindness that reaches beyond the moment. Choosing to lift others isn't just about helping them. It's about creating a pathway to shared growth. By supporting each other's efforts, we rise together and become rooted in resilience, kindness, and mutual respect.

TODAY'S ACTION

Today, take an intentional step to lift a small business in your community. Grab a coffee from a local café, pick up a unique gift from a neighborhood shop, or enjoy a meal at a family-owned restaurant. Go further by leaving a positive review online or sharing your experience on social media. Every small action makes a difference and spreads positivity. Supporting small businesses is more than a transaction. It's an investment in the heart and soul of your community.

TODAY'S AFFIRMATION

I uplift others with love and positive intention.

FEB

MAR

APR

MAY

JUN

JUL

AUG

SEP

OCT

NOV

DEC

RISE BEYOND YOUR PAST

"You may encounter many defeats, but you must not be defeated."

—Maya Angelou

Your past doesn't define you—it strengthens you.
The challenges you've faced and the hardships you've endured are not the end of your story but stepping stones to becoming stronger. Even in moments of deep pain or adversity, resilience lives within you. See it and believe it! Rising beyond your past is about using what you've been through as fuel for growth. Each day, you're becoming a wiser and more empowered version of yourself. You are here to rise!

TODAY'S ACTION

Today, write down one lesson you've learned from a challenging experience, and then reflect on how that lesson has made you stronger or more compassionate. If you're ready, consider sharing this insight with a trusted friend or journaling it to honor your journey. This small act helps to release any lingering pain from the past, letting you move forward with only the lesson it taught you.

TODAY'S AFFIRMATION

I am not my past; I rise with resilience and strength daily.

JAN
FEB
MAR
APR
MAY
JUN
JUL
AUG
SEP
OCT
NOV
DEC

January 10

SPREAD KINDNESS WITH A COMPLIMENT

"A sincere compliment is one of the most effective tools to teach and motivate others."

—ZIG ZIGLAR

A simple compliment can make someone's day shine brighter. In a world that feels rushed and busy, taking a moment to genuinely acknowledge someone's effort, style, or spirit can have a powerful impact. Compliments don't just lift others; they bring more positivity into your life. When you look for the good in others, you train yourself to see the beauty and strength everywhere.

TODAY'S ACTION

Make it a point to share a heartfelt compliment with someone today. Focus on something genuine and specific: their perseverance, talent, or just how they light up the room. You'll be amazed at how a few kind words can transform someone's day and uplift your own heart.

TODAY'S AFFIRMATION

I quickly see and celebrate the beauty in others.

January 11

TURN WORRIES INTO WINS

"Worry never robs tomorrow of its sorrow;
it only saps today of its joy."

—Leo Buscaglia

Gratitude brings you back to the present moment.
Focusing on what's going right instead of what could
go wrong creates space for peace, clarity, and joy. It's
natural to have worries, but letting them control your
thoughts only clouds your ability to see the good around
you. By consciously shifting your mindset from fear to
gratitude, you can transform those anxious moments into
opportunities for growth, resilience, and positivity.

TODAY'S ACTION

The next time you feel worry creeping in, grab a piece of
paper and divide it into two columns. On the left, write
down your top three worries. On the right, write three
things you're grateful for that directly counteract or bring
balance to those worries. For example, if you're worried
about a deadline, you might be thankful for the skills
you've developed to handle challenges. This exercise
shifts your mindset and helps you see how your strengths
and blessings can help you navigate difficult times.

TODAY'S AFFIRMATION

I focus on what's good, and my worries fade away.

FEB

MAR

APR

MAY

JUN

JUL

AUG

SEP

OCT

NOV

DEC

January 12

NOURISH YOUR NERVOUS SYSTEM

"When you regulate your nervous system, you create
a foundation for resilience, joy, and growth."

—MASTIN KIPP

A calm nervous system is the foundation of resilience.
Your nervous system is your body's command center,
orchestrating everything from breathing and heartbeat
to how you respond to stress and joy. Caring for this
complex network deeply influences your physical,
emotional, and mental well-being. By nourishing your
nervous system, you're giving yourself a foundation for
calm, clarity, and greater resilience, helping you handle
life's challenges with ease and positivity.

TODAY'S ACTION

Tonight, choose one calming activity to nourish your
nervous system as you wind down. Try a gentle massage,
slow stretching, sipping herbal tea, or taking deep,
mindful breaths. Focus on each sensation, allowing your
body to relax and recharge fully on a cellular level. This
mindful practice will improve your sleep quality and help
you wake up feeling revitalized.

TODAY'S AFFIRMATION

I nourish my mind and body with calm, care, and
intention.

January 13

LISTEN WITH EMPATHY

"Seek first to understand, then to be understood."

—STEPHEN COVEY

Understanding builds bridges, and bridges bring you closer together. The connection deepens when you focus on finding common ground instead of dwelling on differences. It's easy to feel divided, but genuine connection begins when you listen and seek to understand. By being curious and open-minded, you discover how similar we all are. As we bridge the gap, acquaintances can become friends, and friends turn into family. The more we listen, the more we grow together.

TODAY'S ACTION

In your interactions today, make it a goal to understand the person in front of you truly. Whether a quick chat with a stranger or a deeper conversation with a loved one, focus on listening without judgment. Ask thoughtful questions, find shared experiences, and let the similarities draw you closer. Cultivating this habit will strengthen your bonds and bring more empathy and kindness into your relationships.

TODAY'S AFFIRMATION

I find common ground and build bridges in all my relationships.

January 14

PRACTICE GRATITUDE

"When I started counting my blessings, my whole life turned around."

—WILLIE NELSON

Gratitude is the foundation of abundance and positivity.
It's like a magnet—it draws more of what you appreciate
into your life. The more you give thanks, the more things
you'll find to be grateful for. Consistent gratitude turns
everyday moments into magic. Suddenly, the things you
desire start appearing, opportunities flow your way, and
life deeply supports you.

TODAY'S ACTION

Today, create a gratitude list and aim to add to it
once every hour. Set a timer if you need a reminder.
Wherever you are or whatever you're doing, pause to find
something to appreciate—driving to work? Give thanks
for the journey, your car, or even the coffee in your cup.
Are you making dinner? Appreciate the food, the aromas,
and the ability to nourish yourself and others. By infusing
gratitude into each part of your day, you'll feel a shift
toward greater joy and positivity.

TODAY'S AFFIRMATION

I am grateful for every moment and every blessing that
fills my life.

FEB

MAR

APR

MAY

JUN

JUL

AUG

SEP

OCT

NOV

DEC

FOCUS ON WHAT MATTERS

"Dream big. Start small. But most of all, start."

—Simon Sinek

Big dreams are built on small, focused actions. It's easy to feel overwhelmed when looking at everything you want to accomplish. Still, the secret is breaking it down and prioritizing what matters most. Starting small doesn't diminish your vision; it amplifies it by creating a clear path forward. Focusing on essential tasks makes meaningful progress and builds momentum toward your biggest goals.

TODAY'S ACTION

Go through your to-do list. For each task, ask yourself: Is this essential? Do I want to do it? If not, consider eliminating or delegating it. For basic tasks that don't require your direct involvement, identify who can help—whether it's a friend, a colleague, or a professional you can hire. Write down the name of each person you'll delegate to, and take one immediate step to reach out. Free yourself from tasks that drain your time so you can focus on what matters.

TODAY'S AFFIRMATION

I focus on what matters most, one clear step at a time.

FEB

MAR

APR

MAY

JUN

JUL

AUG

SEP

OCT

NOV

DEC

January 16

GROW THROUGH CHALLENGES

"You don't overcome challenges by making them smaller but by making yourself bigger."

—JOHN MAXWELL

Challenges are opportunities to grow into a stronger version of yourself. Rather than wishing for obstacles to disappear, embrace the chance to expand your capabilities. When you shift your focus from the size of the challenge to your ability to grow through it, you build resilience and confidence. Growth isn't about avoiding challenges but about rising to meet them.

TODAY'S ACTION

Identify a current challenge, big or small. Instead of focusing on how to make it easier, ask yourself, "What can I do to become stronger or more capable?" Write down one skill, mindset, or action to help you confidently tackle this challenge. Start by taking one small step toward building that strength today.

TODAY'S AFFIRMATION

I grow stronger with each challenge I face.

January 17

QUESTION YOUR INNER CRITIC

"You've been criticizing yourself for years, and it hasn't worked. Try approving of yourself and see what happens."

—Louise Hay

Your inner critic isn't helping you reach your best life. It keeps you playing small, focusing on fears instead of possibilities. Accepting its voice without questioning means you're holding yourself back from growth. But each time you challenge it, you take your power back, moving closer to who you are becoming. Questioning your inner critic allows you to rewrite your story and show up fully as yourself.

TODAY'S ACTION

Start to shift how you respond to self-doubt. Identify a situation where your inner critic has been holding you back. Picture this voice as separate from you, and ask yourself, "What would I do if I truly believed in myself?" Then, take one small but bold step in that direction. This simple act of self-approval will help you build confidence and quiet the critic within.

TODAY'S AFFIRMATION

I trust my strengths and believe in my abilities with confidence.

JAN

FEB

MAR

APR

MAY

JUN

JUL

AUG

SEP

OCT

NOV

DEC

January 18

THE POWER OF APPRECIATION

"It doesn't cost you anything to be grateful,
but it could give you everything."

—ELLIE SHOJA

The happiest people focus on what they have, not what they lack. They cultivate gratitude for the present, making their lives feel fuller, richer, and more meaningful. Making gratitude a daily habit shifts your perspective, opening you to more blessings and joy.

TODAY'S ACTION

Set a timer for three moments today—morning, afternoon, and evening. When each timer goes off, take one minute to pause and reflect on something you're grateful for in that moment, like a warm drink, a kind word, or a sense of calm. Jot down a quick note about each reflection. By the end of the day, you'll have a timeline of gratitude to keep you connected to appreciation. Try the *3 Minute Positivity Journal*, which focuses on morning and evening gratitude for greater peace and positivity to stay consistent with a gratitude practice.

TODAY'S AFFIRMATION

I open my heart to appreciation and invite more joy into my life.

January 19

DANCE INTO POSITIVITY

"Get up offa that thing. Dance and you'll feel better."

—JAMES BROWN

Dancing is a celebration that frees your spirit. When you let go and dance, you connect deeply with yourself and tap into positivity. Whether moving to your favorite beat or swaying in silence, dancing releases stress and feels grounding. It opens up to a pure state of happiness. See this joyful act not as a performance but as an expression of your energy, soul, and innate desire for movement.

TODAY'S ACTION

Today, put on a song that lifts your mood and dance like no one's watching. Let your body move in whatever way feels good—no judgments, no holding back. If you feel adventurous, try different music genres or dance styles that are new to you. Feel the joy of dancing and let it remind you of the power of living in the moment.

TODAY'S AFFIRMATION

I embrace freedom and joy as I move to life's rhythm.

FEB

MAR

APR

MAY

JUN

JUL

AUG

SEP

OCT

NOV

DEC

January 20

LIVE FOR TOMORROW

"It is easier to prevent bad habits than to break them."

—Benjamin Franklin

Every habit you form today impacts your future.
Preventing habits that don't serve your vision is a
powerful act of self-care. By choosing habits that
align with your goals now, you're setting yourself up
for a brighter tomorrow instead of being held back by
instant gratification. Your small, intentional daily choices
build a foundation for long-term happiness, resilience,
and success.

TODAY'S ACTION

Take an inventory of your current habits by dividing a
sheet of paper into three columns labeled "Stop," "Start,"
and "Continue." In the "Stop" column, list habits that
hinder your vision. In the "Continue" column, list habits
that support it. Then, in the "Start" column, consider
habits that would bring you closer to your goals if you
adopted them. This reflection helps you see which habits
to nurture and which to release.

TODAY'S AFFIRMATION

I choose habits that bring me happiness and success.

REFLECT AND RECHARGE

"Almost everything will work again if you unplug
it for a few minutes, including you."

—ANNE LAMOTT

Just like a machine needs a reset, so do you. Taking
time to unplug helps you clear mental clutter, recharge
your energy, and reconnect with what matters most.
By intentionally stepping away from life's constant
demands, you create space for fresh insights and
renewed strength to emerge.

TODAY'S ACTION

Set aside 10-15 minutes today for an "unplug" break. Turn
off your phone, step away from screens, and find a quiet
place. Take slow, deep breaths, allowing your mind to
settle. If any insights or reflections arise, jot them down
afterward. Use this moment to recharge, knowing it will
fuel your clarity and energy for what lies ahead.

TODAY'S AFFIRMATION

I take time to unplug, reflect, and recharge, allowing
myself to reset and renew.

FEB

MAR

APR

MAY

JUN

JUL

AUG

SEP

OCT

NOV

DEC

January 22

BREATHE YOUR WAY TO CALM

"Deep breathing changes the chemistry of the body by bringing oxygen into the tissue."

—WIM HOF

If you want to feel better, take deeper breaths. Deep belly breathing expands your diaphragm, filling your lungs fully and bringing much-needed oxygen into your body. This simple practice helps activate your parasympathetic nervous system, which promotes relaxation, lowers stress, and brings a sense of calm. Deep breaths throughout the day can lower blood pressure, ease muscle tension, and even improve digestion. It's a quick, effective way to reconnect with yourself and find tranquility, no matter where you are.

TODAY'S ACTION

Today, give yourself the gift of deep belly breathing. Start by taking at least three slow, deep breaths. Place one hand on your belly and feel it rise as you inhale through your nose, then slowly contract as you exhale through your mouth. Let the air seep in naturally, filling your lungs. Notice how this simple act can shift your energy, clear your mind, and bring you back to a calm place. Practice this throughout the day, and allow it to be your anchor whenever you need clarity and peace.

TODAY'S AFFIRMATION

I breathe in calm and breathe out tension.

January 23

CREATE YOUR SANCTUARY

"The objective of cleaning is not just to clean, but to feel happiness living within that environment."

—MARIE KONDO

A tidy space is a pathway to peace. Your home should be a sanctuary where you feel safe, inspired, and at ease. When your space is free from clutter, it creates room for calm, focus, and positive energy. We overlook the power of a well-kept environment. Still, decluttering is a form of self-care that nourishes both mind and soul. When you invest in your surroundings, you invest in your happiness and well-being.

TODAY'S ACTION

Walk through your home as if seeing it for the first time. Notice each space and how it feels. Spend an hour tidying up with fresh eyes—make the bed, fluff the pillows, clear surfaces, and put away any clutter. Allow yourself to transform your space into a place of peace and inspiration. When you're finished, sit in your favorite spot and soak in the calmness of your fresh, clean sanctuary.

TODAY'S AFFIRMATION

My home is my sanctuary, where I feel happy, peaceful, and inspired.

JAN

FEB

MAR

APR

MAY

JUN

JUL

AUG

SEP

OCT

NOV

DEC

January 24

WELCOME LUCK INTO YOUR LIFE

"I'm lucky. Hard work is the key, but luck plays a part."

—NEIL DIAMOND

When you believe in your luck, you invite positive outcomes into your life. Luck is the outcome of both effort and belief. As neuroscience shows, our thinking shapes our experiences—when we expect good things, we open our minds to opportunities. Each small action you take builds the path to your dreams. You align yourself with possibility, purpose, and positivity by fostering a positive belief in your luck.

TODAY'S ACTION

Take one action toward a goal today, big or small, with the mindset that luck is on your side. Believe that each step has a purpose and that success is within reach. Reflect on how this positive approach enhances your confidence and trust.

TODAY'S AFFIRMATION

I am lucky, and my efforts create positive outcomes.

LOVE IS THE FOUNDATION

"Self-love is the foundation of your mental
and emotional well-being."

—VEX KING

Self-love is essential, not optional. It's self-compassion
and self-respect. Loving yourself creates a ripple that
touches every part of your life. Studies show that self-
compassion reduces stress, boosts resilience, and
elevates happiness. Embracing kindness toward yourself
builds a foundation that lifts your whole life. Treating
yourself with the same love and respect you give others
creates space for pure joy and confidence. It's a chance
to connect deeply with your worth.

TODAY'S ACTION

Today, write yourself a love letter. Find a quiet place,
grab a pen, and jot down three things you appreciate
about yourself. Speak to yourself warmly, as if writing to
a cherished friend. This small act reminds you of your
worth, creating a deeper connection to yourself. As you
strengthen this bond with yourself, you'll find it easier to
welcome love from others with open arms.

TODAY'S AFFIRMATION

I honor my worth and embrace it every day.

INSTANT POSITIVITY **37**

JAN

FEB

MAR

APR

MAY

JUN

JUL

AUG

SEP

OCT

NOV

DEC

January 26

WEALTH STARTS WITH WORTH

"You must gain control over your money, or
the lack of it will forever control you."

—Dave Ramsey

True wealth begins with honoring your worth. Just as managing finances brings freedom, valuing yourself creates inner abundance. When you prioritize self-love and set boundaries, you lay the foundation for confidence, resilience, and lasting joy. Self-worth isn't just about money; it's about investing in the life you deserve.

TODAY'S ACTION

Make a worthy investment. Identify one way to "invest" in yourself today—saying no to what drains you, dedicating time to a passion, or practicing self-compassion. Please write down this act of self-worth and make it a priority. Hold yourself accountable because you're worth it!

TODAY'S AFFIRMATION

I honor my worth and invest in myself with intention.

REFRAME CHALLENGES

"You cannot always control what goes on outside, but you can always control what goes on inside."

—Wayne Dyer

Your mindset is a powerful tool. When you consciously see challenges as opportunities, you transform how you experience life. Studies in cognitive psychology show that reframing challenges reduces stress, strengthens resilience, and boosts mental well-being. By shifting your perspective, you can turn setbacks into stepping stones.

TODAY'S ACTION

The next time a challenge arises, pause and take a deep breath. Notice your initial reaction, then ask yourself, "How can I see this as an opportunity for growth or improvement?" Look for one positive outcome or lesson within the situation. This simple shift can help you move from frustration to a place of possibility.

TODAY'S AFFIRMATION

I am in control of my responses, and I turn challenges into opportunities.

JAN

FEB

MAR

APR

MAY

JUN

JUL

AUG

SEP

OCT

NOV

DEC

January 28

START YOUR DAY WITH HOPE

"If you get up in the morning and think the future will be better, it is a bright day. Otherwise, it's not."

—ELON MUSK

Your outlook in the morning can shape your entire day. When you wake up with a hopeful vision of the future, you invite positivity, energy, and possibility into every moment. This hopeful mindset isn't about ignoring life's challenges—it's about seeing each day as a fresh opportunity to grow, create, and move closer to the life you want. Embracing each morning with optimism sets the foundation for a brighter, more fulfilling day.

TODAY'S ACTION

As soon as you wake up, take a few moments to focus on something you're excited about in the future. Visualize this goal or dream as if it's already happening. Let that hopeful vision fill you with energy and enthusiasm for the day ahead. Notice how this simple practice shifts your mood and sets a positive tone for everything you do.

TODAY'S AFFIRMATION

I start each day with hope and welcome a bright future.

STEP FORWARD IN FAITH

"Faith is taking the first step even when
you don't see the whole staircase."

—Martin Luther King Jr.

Faith invites us to move forward. However uncertain, it's trusting that each step is part of a more powerful journey. It's about trusting that each step leads us closer to where we're meant to be and that we're supported every step of the way. Acting in faith is a choice to believe in what we can't yet see, to trust that we're being guided, and to lean into a plan that may be beyond our understanding. When we embrace faith, we're choosing courage and hope over doubt.

TODAY'S ACTION

Identify one area in your life where you've been holding back. Take a bold step forward today, trusting that God will guide you. Whether making a decision, starting something new, or reaching out to someone, act with full faith and know that the path will reveal itself.

TODAY'S AFFIRMATION

I move forward in faith, trusting that I am guided every step of the way.

FEB

MAR

APR

MAY

JUN

JUL

AUG

SEP

OCT

NOV

DEC

January 30

LET PRAYER LEAD

"Is prayer your steering wheel or your spare tire?"

—CORRIE TEN BOOM

Prayer is meant to guide, not just rescue. Today's quote invites you to reflect: Is prayer the driving force in your life, or just a fallback when things get tough? When prayer leads, it shapes your actions, thoughts, and decisions, grounding you in God's will. By making prayer a core part of your day, you allow it to steer you toward peace, purpose, and a deeper connection with God.

TODAY'S ACTION

Start your day with prayer. Before checking your phone or diving into tasks, dedicate a few quiet moments to connect with God. Ask for guidance, wisdom, and presence. Set an alarm for a midday prayer break to realign your heart and intentions.

TODAY'S AFFIRMATION

I let prayer guide my steps, trusting I am led through each moment.

START WITH WHAT YOU HAVE

"Do what you can, with what you have, where you are."

—THEODORE ROOSEVELT

Growth comes from making the most of where you are right now. You don't need all the answers to begin moving forward. You need to take the next step using the resources and strengths you have right now. Focusing on what you can do today creates progress that builds momentum and moves you closer to your goals.

TODAY'S ACTION

Create a "Quick Start" goal card. Pick one goal that excites you, and write down three specific actions you can take in the next 72 hours to move closer to it. Place the card somewhere visible, and check off each action as you complete it. This card will keep your goal in sight and build powerful momentum.

TODAY'S AFFIRMATION

I create momentum by using what I have to take steps toward my dreams.

February

February 1

CULTIVATE JOY

"A joyful heart is good medicine, but a crushed spirit dries up the bones."

—Proverbs 17:22

Joy is a powerful force that uplifts the soul. Unlike fleeting happiness, joy is a lasting sense of peace and positivity from within, sustained by faith. When we focus on the good in our lives and trust God's presence, we invite joy to take root in our hearts. Joy isn't about ignoring hardships. It's about finding the light even in difficult times, knowing that God's love is constant and unchanging.

TODAY'S ACTION

What brings you joy? Today, take a few moments to focus on answering that question. Reflect on moments when you've felt genuinely grateful or at peace, and write down three things that bring you the most joy. Could you prioritize these this week? Whenever you feel stressed or overwhelmed, return to this list to lift your spirits and refocus on the joy in your life.

TODAY'S AFFIRMATION

My heart is filled with joy, and I radiate positivity and peace.

JAN
FEB
MAR
APR
MAY
JUN
JUL
AUG
SEP
OCT
NOV
DEC

February 2

SWEETEN YOUR LIFE NATURALLY

"Sugar is the tobacco of the new century, a major
cause of obesity and heart disease."

—Dr. Al Sears

Choosing less sugar is choosing better health. Excess
sugar, mainly processed, doesn't just add sweetness—it
adds stress to your body. While natural sugars in fruits
and whole foods nourish, refined sugars can disrupt
health. Studies show that overconsumption of refined
sugar is linked to issues like obesity, diabetes, heart
disease, and chronic inflammation. You're taking charge
of your physical health by cutting back and boosting
mental clarity and mood.

TODAY'S ACTION

Take a closer look at your sugar intake today. Start
by reading food labels and choosing options without
added sugars. Swap sugary drinks for water with lemon
or herbal tea, and try natural sweets like fruit to satisfy
cravings. Each small choice adds significant health
benefits, keeping you energized, clear-headed, and
naturally optimistic.

TODAY'S AFFIRMATION

I choose nourishing foods that support my body
and mind.

February 3

MAKE TIME TO PAMPER YOURSELF

"Self-care is giving the world the best of you, instead of what's left of you."

—KATIE REED

Pampering yourself is essential to your well-being. In a world always demanding more, taking time to nurture yourself might feel indulgent—but it's actually about refilling your cup. When you prioritize self-care, you boost your energy and create a positive ripple that benefits everyone around you. When you feel rested and cared for, you can show up with more joy, calm, and positivity.

TODAY'S ACTION

Plan a small act of pampering today. It could be a warm bath, an at-home facial, a leisurely walk, or simply setting aside time to read or listen to music. Whatever you choose, let this time entirely focus on you and what brings you peace. For more daily self-care inspiration, check out the free challenge at 7daysofselfcare.com and make positivity a habit.

TODAY'S AFFIRMATION

I take time to nourish my mind, body, and soul.

JAN
FEB
MAR
APR
MAY
JUN
JUL
AUG
SEP
OCT
NOV
DEC

February 4

MAKE SPACE TO PAUSE

"You are worth the quiet moment. You are worth the deeper breath. You are worth the time it takes to slow down, be still, and rest."

—MORGAN HARPER NICHOLS

Your mental health is the foundation of everything.
Taking time to pause isn't just a break—it's a necessity. When you allow yourself to pause, you create space for calm, clarity, and renewal. Just as you would rest to heal physically, dedicating time for a mental pause allows your mind to recharge and realign with what matters most.

TODAY'S ACTION

Prioritize a day to pause and rejuvenate. If today isn't an option, choose an upcoming date, mark it on your calendar, and let others know you're taking a mental health day. Plan moments that help you pause and reset, whether that's time in nature, a peaceful afternoon with a book, or simply resting. Let this be a gift to yourself, knowing it will restore your energy and help you return to life with clarity and strength.

TODAY'S AFFIRMATION

I make space to pause and renew my mental well-being.

February 5

LIGHTEN YOUR HEART

"Growth is painful. Change is painful. But nothing is as painful as staying stuck somewhere you don't belong."

—MANDY HALE

Grudges are a heavy weight that drains your energy and growth. Think about the grudge that lingers in your mind—the one that stirs up anger whenever it crosses your thoughts. Has holding onto it brought you joy or peace? Most likely, it's weighed you down, making it harder to welcome new opportunities. Grudges don't punish others; they punish you. Letting go isn't about excusing someone's actions. It's about reclaiming your freedom and opening your heart to new growth.

TODAY'S ACTION

Today, let go of one grudge and feel the freedom of lightening your heart. Imagine this grudge as a heavy backpack you've been carrying for far too long. Picture yourself setting it down or giving it to God. Then, feel the wave of relief. Write down what you're ready to release, take a deep breath, and say, "I choose peace over resentment." This simple yet powerful act is for you. It's time to make room for joy, peace, and positivity.

TODAY'S AFFIRMATION

I release past hurts and make room for new growth.

INSTANT POSITIVITY   **49**

JAN

FEB

MAR

APR

MAY

JUN

JUL

AUG

SEP

OCT

NOV

DEC

February 6

SOAK THE DAY AWAY

"Anyone who thinks heaven is not hot water behind a locked door has forgotten what it means to live."

—LUCY FRANK

A warm bath can be a sanctuary for both body and mind. Taking a moment to soak in warm water can do wonders for your muscles, mind, and mood. The heat relaxes your muscles, improves circulation, and creates a sense of calm that allows you to unwind from the day's demands. Bath time isn't just about relaxation; it's about giving yourself permission to rest, reset, and recharge. As you soak, let go of the tension, the stress, and anything weighing you down.

TODAY'S ACTION

Create a mini spa experience by drawing yourself a warm bath. Add Epsom salts, essential oils, or even a touch of magnesium for extra nourishment. Dim the lights, light a candle, and put on some calming music. Allow yourself to unwind fully, focusing on each breath and letting the warm water melt away your worries. Give yourself permission to fully enjoy this time—because, friend, you deserve it.

TODAY'S AFFIRMATION

I am worthy of rest and renewal.

GIVE BACK WITH HEART

"Service to others is the rent you pay for your room here on earth."

—Muhammad Ali

Volunteering isn't just an act of giving—it's an exchange of humanity. Studies show that giving back uplifts others, reduces stress, boosts mood, and increases life satisfaction. When we lend a hand, we experience a "helper's high," reinforcing positive emotions and a sense of fulfillment. Every act of kindness—no matter how small—builds bridges, fosters unity, and reminds us of the goodness in the world. When we serve with an open heart, we create ripples of positivity that reach far beyond our lives.

TODAY'S ACTION

Today, find a way to give back, whether big or small. Look for a local charity, offer to serve meals, plant trees, lend a listening ear, or help a needy neighbor. Each act of kindness—large or small—leaves a ripple that builds humanity and spreads positivity.

TODAY'S AFFIRMATION

As I serve others, I bring love into my own heart.

FEB

MAR

APR

MAY

JUN

JUL

AUG

SEP

OCT

NOV

DEC

February 8

AUTHENTICITY THROUGH VULNERABILITY

"Staying vulnerable is a risk we have to take if we want to experience connection."

—BRENÉ BROWN

Choosing vulnerability is choosing to live authentically. When we are vulnerable, we open up to deeper connections and invite genuine, meaningful relationships into our lives. Vulnerability can feel risky, but we find authentic connection and acceptance through this openness. Embracing authenticity means showing up as our true selves, unafraid of imperfection, and trusting that those who matter will see our worth and respond with compassion and understanding.

TODAY'S ACTION

Today, take a small step towards authentic vulnerability. Think of one thing you haven't shared with a close friend, family member, or partner—a thought, feeling, or story that reflects your true self. Open up to them with honesty and notice how it feels. This practice strengthens bonds and reinforces your confidence in showing up as the real you!

TODAY'S AFFIRMATION

I embrace my true self with confidence and courage.

THE POWER OF CUDDLING

"Cuddling with you feels like touching the stars."

—GIOVANNIE DE SADELEER

Few things are as comforting as a good cuddle. You create a haven of warmth and connection when you snuggle with a loved one, whether a partner, child, or close friend. Science shows that cuddling releases oxytocin—the "love hormone"—which reduces stress, lowers blood pressure, and fosters feelings of trust and affection. These small moments of closeness remind us of the beauty and importance of human connection!

TODAY'S ACTION

Today, make space for a cuddle. If you can, embrace a partner or a loved one. If that isn't possible, try cuddling with a pet or wrapping yourself in a cozy blanket, allowing the softness to comfort you. Even a long hug from a friend or family member can provide the same sense of belonging. And if none of these options are available, consider opening your life to relationships that allow for this kind of connection.

TODAY'S AFFIRMATION

I am grateful for the warmth and love in my life.

JAN
FEB
MAR
APR
MAY
JUN
JUL
AUG
SEP
OCT
NOV
DEC

February 10

SPREAD LOVE THROUGH LETTERS

"Writing a letter is the next best thing to showing
up personally at someone's door."

—Shannon L. Alder

Plant a seed of joy in someone's heart. In today's digital
world, handwritten letters carry a special kind of magic.
The time you take to write, the thought behind each word,
and the uniqueness of your handwriting transform a
simple note into a heartfelt gift. A letter holds a piece of
you—your kindness, thoughtfulness, and care. Whether
it's to say "thank you," "I miss you," or "I'm thinking of
you," sending a letter can deepen your connection with
someone, even across great distances.

TODAY'S ACTION

When was the last time you sent a handwritten note?
Today, pick someone special and write them a letter.
Choose beautiful stationery, a card, or a simple sheet
of paper. Pour your love, gratitude, or encouragement
onto the page, then seal it and send it with a smile. To
deepen this action, consider writing a note to someone
you haven't spoken to or even a child or elderly family
member who would love this personal touch.

TODAY'S AFFIRMATION

I share my love and care in thoughtful ways.

February 11

CONNECT THROUGH CONVERSATION

"Communication works for those who work at it."

—JOHN POWELL

Every conversation is an opportunity for connection.
When you engage with someone thoughtfully, you
build trust and foster a sense of belonging. Authentic
connection comes from mindful, intentional dialogue—
showing up with curiosity, empathy, and a genuine interest
in what the other person has to share. Communication is a
skill that deepens with practice, creating bonds that uplift
and strengthen our relationships.

TODAY'S ACTION

Today, try this conversation challenge. Choose one person
you'd like to connect with more deeply. Set aside at least
10 minutes for an uninterrupted conversation. During this
time, be fully present: listen actively, ask open-ended
questions, and offer reflections that show understanding.
Let the goal be a connection, not just exchanging words.
Notice how this mindful interaction strengthens your bond
and makes you feel more understood.

TODAY'S AFFIRMATION

I nurture my relationships through authentic and mindful
conversations.

JAN

FEB

MAR

APR

MAY

JUN

JUL

AUG

SEP

OCT

NOV

DEC

February 12

GIVE WITH PURPOSE

"Giving is not just about making a donation.
It's about making a difference."

—Kathy Calvin

Giving with purpose is a gift that lifts everyone. True generosity goes beyond simply offering material things; it's about sharing a piece of yourself with those around you. Choosing to give reminds us of our interconnectedness in a world that focuses on individual success. When we contribute intentionally, we foster a spirit of community that grows beyond giving.

TODAY'S ACTION

Take a moment to consider what you can give with purpose today. Look around your home for items you no longer need that might bring value to someone else—perhaps a book that inspired you, clothing that no longer serves you, or a well-loved piece of furniture. You might also consider donating your time or sharing a skill with someone who would value it. Whatever you choose, reflect on how giving can brighten someone's day and fill your heart with gratitude.

TODAY'S AFFIRMATION

I live with purpose, contributing to a more positive world.

February 13

SPREAD KINDNESS LIKE SUNSHINE

"Remember, there's no such thing as a small act of kindness.
Every act creates a ripple with no logical end."

—Scott Adams

Kindness is a gift that brightens every corner it touches.
It uplifts, heals, and transforms both the giver and the
receiver. Kindness is a powerful choice that creates
positive change in a world that can feel overwhelming.
Even the smallest acts—a warm smile, a kind word, or a
helping hand—can create a ripple effect, reaching further
than we may ever know. Imagine a world where kindness
is the default. By choosing kindness, you shine your light
and help build that world one moment at a time.

TODAY'S ACTION

Today, make kindness a habit. Set an intention to perform
at least three acts of kindness—big or small—before
the day ends. You could try complimenting a stranger,
paying for someone's coffee, or sending an encouraging
message to a friend. Be mindful and intentional with each
gesture, noticing how it not only lifts others but also fills
you with positivity. To keep the momentum going, consider
keeping a kindness journal, noting each day how you
showed kindness and the difference it made in your day.

TODAY'S AFFIRMATION

I choose to spread kindness like sunshine.

INSTANT POSITIVITY **57**

JAN

FEB

MAR

APR

MAY

JUN

JUL

AUG

SEP

OCT

NOV

DEC

February 14

LOVE THY NEIGHBOR

"Let all that you do be done in love."

—1 Corinthians 16:14

Love is a gift meant to be shared with everyone we meet. It isn't just reserved for romantic relationships—it's woven into our daily lives and the small acts of kindness we share. Remember that we don't need a partner to make it special or meaningful on this day of love. No matter how small, every connection can uplift, inspire, and spread warmth. By showing love today and every day, we create a ripple of joy that reaches further than we imagine.

TODAY'S ACTION

Today, celebrate love by connecting with someone in your neighborhood or community. Bring a small gift, write a kind note, or stop by for a friendly chat. Consider calling or sending a thoughtful message if an in-person visit isn't possible. This simple gesture can bring joy, spark friendships, and remind both of you that love shines brightest in everyday moments.

TODAY'S AFFIRMATION

I am surrounded by love and share it with those around me.

February 15

GRATEFUL WORDS, HAPPY HEARTS

"Feeling gratitude and not expressing it is like wrapping a present and not giving it."

—William Arthur Ward

Gratitude is a gift that becomes even more meaningful when shared. Expressing thanks has a positive impact both on those who give it and those who receive it. When you take a moment to acknowledge someone's kindness, it shows them they're valued and seen, creating a ripple of joy and connection. Imagine how much brighter the world would feel if we expressed our gratitude freely.

TODAY'S ACTION

Today, list three people who have positively impacted your life, whether recently or in the past. Write each of them a heartfelt thank-you note. It doesn't have to be lengthy—a few sincere words of appreciation go a long way. Choose a particular card, a simple note, or a sticky note. If mailing isn't an option, consider delivering it in person or snapping a photo to text it. This simple gesture of gratitude brings joy to their day. It deepens your connection, inspiring more appreciation in both your lives.

TODAY'S AFFIRMATION

I express my gratitude and spread joy to those around me.

JAN

FEB

MAR

APR

MAY

JUN

JUL

AUG

SEP

OCT

NOV

DEC

February 16

GROW KINDNESS

"A single act of kindness throws out roots in all directions, and the roots spring up and make new trees."

—AMELIA EARHART

Kindness is a seed that blossoms into endless beauty.
Each kind of act, no matter how small, carries the potential to uplift, inspire, and transform. Kindness connects us, weaving a web of positivity that strengthens our communities and spirits. Imagine each act as planting a seed that will grow and extend its branches, reaching others in ways you may never see. By choosing kindness, you're building a legacy of compassion that can ripple through lives far beyond your own.

TODAY'S ACTION

Start a daily kindness habit today. Commit to at least one intentional act of kindness every day this week. It could be leaving a kind note for a coworker, paying for someone's coffee, or listening deeply to someone who needs it. Each small gesture nurtures positivity, growing connections, and warmth in ways that benefit everyone. Let today be the beginning of a practice that becomes second nature.

TODAY'S AFFIRMATION

I plant seeds of kindness that grow far and wide.

February 17

EMBRACE YOUR WORTHINESS

"As I began to love myself, I freed myself of anything that is no good for my health—food, people, things, situations, and everything that drew me down and away from myself."

—CHARLIE CHAPLIN

Sometimes, the love we seek begins with ourselves. Learning to love yourself may initially feel unusual, but it's a powerful reminder that you carry strength and confidence within. When you treat yourself compassionately, you affirm your worth and reinforce the belief that you deserve kindness. These moments create a foundation of resilience and positivity, empowering you to show up fully and authentically in every part of your life.

TODAY'S ACTION

Today, whenever you need a reminder of your worth, take a moment to hug yourself. Wrap your arms around yourself, close your eyes, and take a deep, steady breath. As you exhale, whisper a phrase of affirmation like, "I am worthy" or "I am enough." Let each warm embrace remind you of the inner strength and beauty you hold. For an extra boost, try standing in front of a mirror, appreciating the person you're becoming daily.

TODAY'S AFFIRMATION

I am enough, and I love myself unconditionally.

JAN
FEB
MAR
APR
MAY
JUN
JUL
AUG
SEP
OCT
NOV
DEC

February 18

READ WITH INTENTION

"The right book at the right time could change your life."

—Nick Hutchison

Books are powerful tools for growth. When you read with intention, you're absorbing information and inviting transformation. Studies show that purposeful reading can reduce stress, increase empathy, and enhance well-being. The right book at the right time can provide precisely the wisdom, clarity, or encouragement you need to take the next step forward.

TODAY'S ACTION

Think about a challenge or area of your life you'd like to improve. Please take a few minutes to search for books that align with this need and order it. If you're unsure where to start, reach out to @bookthinkers on Instagram—Nick Hutchison and his team love to recommend books that fit your goals. Embrace the power of intentional reading, and watch how it inspires new ideas and action steps in your life.

TODAY'S AFFIRMATION

I choose books with intention; knowing the right book at the right time can change my life.

February 19

HEAL YOUR GUT, TRUST YOUR GUT

"A healthy gut is a foundation for a healthy mind.
Listen to what your gut is telling you."

—DR. JOSH AXE

A healthy gut is the cornerstone of a healthy mind.
Your gut does more than digest food; it influences your
mood, reduces anxiety, and enhances brain function. The
"second brain" communicates with your mind through
the gut-brain axis, sending signals that shape your well-
being. Trusting your gut isn't just a saying—it's rooted in
science, profoundly connecting your body and mind. How
amazing is that?

TODAY'S ACTION

Reflect on your recent food choices. Are there small
changes you can make to support a healthier gut?
Consider adding more fiber-rich foods and probiotics or
simply drinking more water. Notice how your body feels
after different meals, and use this awareness to make
choices that nourish your gut. Trust that listening to your
gut can lead to a healthier mind and body.

TODAY'S AFFIRMATION

I nourish my gut and trust its wisdom to support my
well-being.

JAN

FEB

MAR

APR

MAY

JUN

JUL

AUG

SEP

OCT

NOV

DEC

February 20

HONOR YOUR COMMITMENTS

"We are what we repeatedly do. Excellence,
then, is not an act, but a habit."

—ARISTOTLE

Honoring your commitments is at the heart of integrity.
Every time you follow through on your promises to
yourself, you reinforce a foundation of trust and inner
strength. These small acts of consistency build a resilient
character, reminding you of your power to grow and
evolve. By staying true to your goals, you create a ripple
effect of positivity and set a standard of excellence for
yourself and those around you.

TODAY'S ACTION

Identify one commitment you've made to yourself,
and honor it fully today. Whether exercising, eating
mindfully, or spending less time on social media, take
one clear, intentional step to keep that promise. Notice
how this choice boosts your confidence and strengthens
your resolve.

TODAY'S AFFIRMATION

I honor my commitments to myself, building integrity and
strength every day.

LET FAITH BE YOUR STRENGTH

"Faith is the strength by which a shattered
world shall emerge into the light."

—HELEN KELLER

Faith is the light that guides you through dark times.
It's the quiet assurance that, even when everything feels
broken, there's still an opportunity waiting for you. Faith
helps you rise from challenges. It gives you the courage
to move forward. It reminds you that there's meaning
and growth on the other side. Every struggle has the
potential to lead you toward greater strength, clarity, and
positivity. Believe it!

TODAY'S ACTION

Take a step today to strengthen your faith. Find a quiet
space, close your eyes, and reflect on one challenge
you're facing. Visualize yourself stronger on the other
side, filled with hope and resilience. Say a prayer, set an
intention, or write down one positive outcome you choose
to believe in despite the circumstances. Let this act of
faith empower you to keep moving forward.

TODAY'S AFFIRMATION

My faith will lead me through challenges and into light.

JAN
FEB
MAR
APR
MAY
JUN
JUL
AUG
SEP
OCT
NOV
DEC

February 22

CELEBRATE YOUR BEAUTY

"Beauty is not what you look like. It's what you are like and who you are."

—DREW BARRYMORE

True beauty radiates from within, reflecting kindness, authenticity, and self-respect. When we focus on what we are like rather than what we look like, we tap into a beauty that's timeless. It's easy to get caught up in appearances. The truth is that the qualities that make us beautiful come from the inside. Embracing this perspective allows us to see ourselves in a gentler light. It allows us to honor who we are and the skin we're in.

TODAY'S ACTION

Today, write down three qualities you genuinely admire in yourself that reflect who you are at your best. Once you've listed them, choose one quality to embody throughout the day. Let it guide your thoughts and actions. This simple practice brings your inner beauty to the surface, gently reminding you that your worth goes far beyond appearances.

TODAY'S AFFIRMATION

I celebrate my inner beauty and the light I bring to the world.

February 23

OWN YOUR HONESTY

"Honesty is the first chapter in the book of wisdom."

—THOMAS JEFFERSON

Being truthful with yourself and others is a cornerstone of growth. Honesty creates a foundation for trust, respect, and stronger connections. Honesty isn't always easy, especially if it might hurt someone, but it opens the door to growth and healing. Even when it's challenging, choosing honesty shows courage and commitment to living with integrity.

TODAY'S ACTION

Reflect on an area where honesty could spark positive change. Is there a conversation you've been avoiding, an overdue apology, or a truth you need to face within? Today, take one step toward embracing honesty— whether it's speaking up, saying sorry, or acknowledging your feelings. Feel the lightness from being true to yourself and notice how it strengthens your bonds with others.

TODAY'S AFFIRMATION

I embrace honesty and grow in wisdom every day.

FEB

MAR

APR

MAY

JUN

JUL

AUG

SEP

OCT

NOV

DEC

February 24

MEND WITH MEANING

"Apologizing doesn't mean you're wrong; it means you value the relationship more than your pride."

—MARK MATTHEWS

Genuine connection grows from the courage to make things right. Taking steps to mend a relationship is one of the most powerful ways to show someone they matter. Genuine connection grows when we set aside ego and let love lead the way. Apologizing isn't always about who is right or wrong. It's about creating space for healing and showing that the relationship is more important than any disagreement. Apologizing deepens our understanding and brings us closer together.

TODAY'S ACTION

Today, think of a relationship that could benefit from an apology, even to clear the air. Reach out with an open heart, ready to bridge the gap. Start by recognizing the other person's feelings and express your desire to restore harmony. Notice how this act of kindness restores peace, warmth, and meaning in your lives.

TODAY'S AFFIRMATION

I mend my relationships with love and an open heart.

NOURISH YOUR HEART

"Small dietary changes can have significant impacts on mental well-being."

—DR. UMA NAIDOO

Small choices make a big difference to well-being.
Your heart is more than an organ—it's the rhythm of your life, supporting every function and connection in your body. Prioritizing heart health has a ripple effect on your energy, mood, and mental clarity. Choosing heart-healthy snacks gives you the nutrients to boost mental well-being and physical vitality. Every heart-smart bite is an act of love toward yourself, fueling you to live fully and feel your best.

TODAY'S ACTION

Stock up on a variety of heart-healthy snacks, like nuts, seeds, fresh fruits, and colorful veggies. Place a bowl of fruits or a jar of nuts within easy reach to encourage nourishing choices throughout your day. Notice how these snacks lift your mood and energize you, knowing that every bite strengthens and supports your body's rhythm.

TODAY'S AFFIRMATION

I nourish my body with love and mindful choices.

JAN

FEB

MAR

APR

MAY

JUN

JUL

AUG

SEP

OCT

NOV

DEC

February 26

CHOOSE TO BE EXTRAORDINARY

"It is possible for ordinary people to choose to be extraordinary."

—Elon Musk

Every extraordinary journey starts with a simple choice. It's not talent or luck that makes the difference—it's the decision to push beyond the ordinary. When you choose to be extraordinary, you commit to growth, resilience, and taking bold steps toward your potential. Success isn't about following a formula; it's about believing in yourself and showing up every day. You don't need a perfect plan—just a willingness to grow and make each day count.

TODAY'S ACTION

Expand your comfort zone with an "Extraordinary Action." Choose one goal you've been hesitant about, and take a bold step toward it. Pick something that feels ambitious yet exciting. Let this action ignite your journey toward greatness, whether reaching out to a mentor, learning a new skill, starting a project, or setting a personal best.

TODAY'S AFFIRMATION

I choose to be extraordinary and take bold steps towards my highest potential.

February 27

BELIEVE IN YOURSELF

"Stop trying to find the formula. Success is about self-belief and persistence."

—Sara Blakely

Success doesn't come with a perfect formula. Instead, it's built from trusting in yourself and pushing forward, even when the path isn't clear. Believing in your vision and staying persistent, regardless of setbacks, sets you apart. Trust that you already have what it takes to make your dreams happen—what matters most is the commitment to keep going.

TODAY'S ACTION

Today, take one bold step forward to pursue your goal without worrying if it's perfect. Send that email, pitch the idea, or start the project you've been holding off. Embrace this step confidently, knowing every action brings you closer to your vision.

TODAY'S AFFIRMATION

I trust in myself and keep moving forward with purpose.

INSTANT POSITIVITY **71**

JAN
FEB
MAR
APR
MAY
JUN
JUL
AUG
SEP
OCT
NOV
DEC

February 28

LEAD WITH COMPASSION

"Compassion is the language the deaf can hear and the blind can see."

—Mark Twain

Compassion is the bridge that connects our hearts. It's the quiet, gentle act of seeing another person and letting them know they matter. When you lead with compassion, you create a ripple of kindness that can touch lives in ways words alone can't. It's about opening your heart and showing up for others, even in small, simple ways. When you respond with compassion, you're not just uplifting others—you're filling your life with warmth, connection, and purpose. Letting your heart lead makes the world a kinder, more understanding place.

TODAY'S ACTION

Bring a little extra compassion to your day! Whether it's offering a compliment, holding the door open, or simply giving someone your full attention, let your heart lead the way. Smile, listen, and share your kindness generously. Even small acts can create big, beautiful ripples of positivity.

TODAY'S AFFIRMATION

I open my heart with compassion and let it guide my actions.

February 29

STAY ROOTED, STAY STRONG

"The more grounded you are, the higher you can soar. Grounding is the foundation of growth and expansion."

—TONY ROBBINS

The deeper your roots, the stronger you grow. Grounding is a practice that anchors your energy, fosters stability and keeps you connected to the present moment. Especially during times of stress and uncertainty, grounding can help you find clarity, peace, and strength. Standing barefoot on the Earth can help you feel more centered. It's a reminder that no matter how chaotic life gets, you have the power to stay grounded, calm, and steady.

TODAY'S ACTION

Start your day by grounding yourself. Step outside and walk barefoot on grass, sand, or soil if possible. Feel the texture and temperature beneath your feet and take a few deep breaths. If you're indoors, sit comfortably with your feet flat on the floor. Close your eyes, take a few deep breaths, and focus on the sensation of your feet connected to the ground. This simple practice can help you reset, find calm, and stay positive throughout your day.

TODAY'S AFFIRMATION

I am grounded, calm, and at peace.

March

March 1

CHOOSE POSITIVITY

"Positivity isn't just a mood; it's a practice that shapes your reality."

—KRISTEN BUTLER

Positivity is a choice and a habit. It's more than mindset; it's a lifestyle. When you consciously focus on the good, you create a ripple effect that impacts every area of your life. Embracing positivity doesn't mean ignoring life's challenges—it means approaching them with resilience, gratitude, and an open heart. By cultivating a daily positivity practice, you build a foundation of joy and strength that empowers you to handle anything with grace and confidence.

TODAY'S ACTION

Create a simple positivity ritual to start each day. Write down three things you're grateful for, recite an uplifting affirmation, or spend a few minutes envisioning a positive outcome for the day ahead. Make this your own, and commit to it for the month to see how it lifts your mood, mindset, and energy. If it resonates, consider sharing this new practice with someone you know to hold you accountable and to spread the ripple of positivity!

TODAY'S AFFIRMATION

I choose positivity every day to create a brighter future.

JAN
FEB
MAR
APR
MAY
JUN
JUL
AUG
SEP
OCT
NOV
DEC

March 2

HARNESS THE POWER OF YOUR THOUGHTS

"Thoughts become things. If you can see it in your mind, you can hold it in your hand."

—DR. JOE DISPENZA

Your thoughts are powerful—each one shapes the reality you experience. When you direct your thoughts with intention, you're creating a blueprint for the life you desire. By focusing on positive possibilities, you attract situations and experiences that align with your vision. This is more than wishful thinking; it's a mindset shift that can transform how you see the world and how the world responds to you.

TODAY'S ACTION

Start a "Thought-to-Reality" sticky note habit. Write down a specific future reality you're working toward, like "I am a bestselling author," "I am financially free," or "I have a dream career." Place this sticky note somewhere you'll see it consistently, like on your mirror or laptop. Each time you see it, take a moment to visualize this reality and feel the excitement as if it's already true.

TODAY'S AFFIRMATION

I shape my reality by focusing on thoughts that align with my highest vision.

March 3

EMBRACE YOUR IMPERFECTIONS

"Success is not final, failure is not fatal: It is the courage to continue that counts."

—Winston Churchill

Grace is the gift we give ourselves. Growth is a journey, not a race. Being gentle with yourself opens room for authenticity, courage, and resilience. When you allow yourself to be imperfect, you create space for growth and build the foundation for self-love. Showing yourself grace means treating yourself with the same kindness you offer a friend, learning from mistakes, and recognizing that every experience moves you closer to who you're meant to be.

TODAY'S ACTION

Today, try something you've wanted to do but held back from because of fear of failure. Whether it's a new skill, hobby, or goal, embrace the chance to grow without expecting perfection. Dive in with curiosity and a playful spirit, knowing that each attempt—no matter the outcome—brings you closer to confidence, resilience, and joy.

TODAY'S AFFIRMATION

I am worthy of grace and kindness from myself.

JAN

FEB

MAR

APR

MAY

JUN

JUL

AUG

SEP

OCT

NOV

DEC

March 4

STRENGTHEN YOUR CIRCLE

"We are wired for connection, and connection gives purpose and meaning to our lives."

—Brené Brown

Connection is the heart of a fulfilling life. Nurturing meaningful relationships creates a network of support, joy, and shared experiences that uplift everyone. Building connections isn't about the quantity of relationships but the quality, where empathy, trust, and kindness lay the foundation. Every relationship you invest in adds richness to your life and reminds you that you're part of something bigger. Genuine connection fuels your positivity and growth.

TODAY'S ACTION

Challenge yourself to elevate a connection by bringing quality and intention to your interactions. Choose one person you want to connect with on a deeper level and reach out to them with a question or topic that shows genuine interest in their life or dreams. Go beyond surface-level conversation—ask about their latest passion, a recent challenge, or something they're proud of. If possible, make plans for a meaningful activity together. Notice how focusing on the quality of this connection adds depth to your relationship.

TODAY'S AFFIRMATION

I am open to connection and nurturing relationships that uplift my life.

March 5

PRACTICE EVENING GRATITUDE

"Choosing to be positive and having a grateful attitude is going to determine how you're going to live your life."

—JOEL OSTEEN

Gratitude is the key to living a life you love. When you choose gratitude, you shift your focus from what's lacking to what's abundant, creating more positivity. Every day holds countless moments of goodness, even if they seem small, and it's easy to overlook them when stress or a challenge takes center stage. By practicing evening gratitude, you can wrap up your day on a high note, reflecting on the good and training your mind to see abundance over lack. This simple habit invites more of what you love into your life for daily growth.

TODAY'S ACTION

Before bed tonight, take a moment to list three things you're grateful for from the day. Did something make you laugh out loud? Did you have a delicious meal? Please write it down, and let those warm feelings settle in as you drift off to sleep. You'll end the day with a smile and wake up ready to take on the world!

TODAY'S AFFIRMATION

I end my day with peace, positivity, and gratitude.

JAN

FEB

MAR

APR

MAY

JUN

JUL

AUG

SEP

OCT

NOV

DEC

March 6

ELEVATE YOUR LANGUAGE

"Words are things. You must be careful…
they can be used for good or ill."

—MAYA ANGELOU

Our words shape our reality. Every word you choose has
the power to create to dim, to inspire, or to discourage.
You attract more joy, opportunity, and meaningful
connections when you become intentional with positive
language. Choosing words that reflect kindness,
gratitude, and hope transforms your day, helping you see
the good even when it's hard. Elevating your language
is more than a habit—it's a practice that nurtures self-
respect and empowerment.

TODAY'S ACTION

Challenge yourself to use only positive words today. If
you catch yourself about to complain, stop and reframe
it into something constructive. Share encouraging
words with others and choose language that uplifts your
spirit. As you end the day, take a moment to reflect on
how choosing positivity has influenced your mood and
outlook. Consider how this change can help you build
stronger, healthier relationships, starting with yourself.

TODAY'S AFFIRMATION

I choose words that uplift, inspire, and create positivity.

March 7

EMBRACE SELF-FORGIVENESS

"Forgive yourself first. Release the need to replay a
negative situation over and over again in your mind."

—LES BROWN

Forgiveness is freedom. It's a gift you give yourself. When
you forgive yourself, you release the weight of regret
and self-criticism, opening the door to growth. It creates
space for healing, allowing love and compassion to
replace blame. By forgiving yourself, you free up energy
to focus on the things that truly matter, nurturing a heart
that's open and ready for happiness.

TODAY'S ACTION

If you've been carrying the weight of self-judgment,
today is the day to lighten that load. Take a moment to
reflect on any lingering regrets or harsh judgments. Write
a letter to yourself, acknowledging mistakes and offering
compassion, understanding, and forgiveness. Let this be
a turning point to release old burdens, knowing that every
day is a new chance to begin again with kindness.

TODAY'S AFFIRMATION

I let go of past mistakes and forgive myself fully.

FEB

MAR

APR

MAY

JUN

JUL

AUG

SEP

OCT

NOV

DEC

March 8

TURN YOUR DREAM INTO REALITY

"It's not an experiment if you know it's going to work."

—JEFF BEZOS

True innovation begins with a leap of faith. When you pursue your dreams, the outcome is sometimes uncertain. Progress is taking bold steps forward. Realizing your vision is about more than just knowing every answer. It's about trusting the process, learning from each step, and staying focused on the big picture. Let your passion fuel you. Even when the path feels unclear, each step will take you closer to what's possible.

TODAY'S ACTION

Identify one goal or vision you've hesitated to start because of uncertainty. Please write down the first small step you can take toward it today. Commit to this step, and as you move forward, trust that clarity will come with action. Growth happens when you push beyond the comfort of certainty.

TODAY'S AFFIRMATION

I trust my vision and take bold steps toward making it a reality.

March 9

EMBRACE TRUE FREEDOM

"True freedom is not the ability to do whatever we want, but to become all that God intends us to be."

—JOHN PIPER

True freedom is about becoming who you are meant to be. It's the courage to step into your purpose and the wisdom to let go of distractions. When you align with God's plan, you're free and empowered. Every choice you make with intention moves you closer to a life of meaning, strength, and fulfillment.

TODAY'S ACTION

Identify one commitment, habit, or responsibility that feels like it's weighing you down or doesn't serve your purpose. Today, Take a bold step to delegate, reduce, or remove it from your life. Freeing up this space allows you to focus more on the path God has intended for you, giving you more room to grow and live with intention.

TODAY'S AFFIRMATION

I am free to grow into all that God intends for me.

March 10

STEP INTO POSITIVITY

"Optimism is the faith that leads to achievement."

—HELEN KELLER

Every great accomplishment begins with a single step of belief. When you let go of doubt and lean into possibility, you unlock doors you may not have known existed. You hold a unique potential within you that's waiting to be discovered—your dreams, strengths, and talents are all seeds of greatness, ready to grow. Embracing possibility is about trusting that the path will unfold as you walk it, knowing that each small action takes you closer to a future filled with purpose, growth, and positivity.

TODAY'S ACTION

Pick one goal you've been holding back on. Write it down and visualize it as if it's already happening. Then, take a bold, clear step today to make it real. Your next step could be reaching out to someone who inspires you, carving out 10 minutes to brainstorm your next move, or setting a reminder that keeps you on track. Each small action is a promise to yourself and a powerful momentum builder—start now and feel the shift!

TODAY'S AFFIRMATION

I trust in new possibilities and step forward with positivity.

March 11

LIVE WITH JOY

"Joy is the serious business of heaven."

—C.S. Lewis

Joy is a source of strength and purpose. It's more than just an emotion. When you embrace joy, you elevate your well-being and find meaning daily. Joy fuels your resilience, keeps you grounded, and brings light to others. Choosing joy is an investment in your peace and the happiness of those around you. Living with joy means appreciating the beauty in simple things and trusting that each moment holds something to be grateful for.

TODAY'S ACTION

Today, bring a sense of joy into everything you do. Start with a small act that uplifts you—a favorite song, a moment of gratitude, or a walk outside. Notice how this shifts your mood and fills you with energy. Let joy guide your day and influence every part of your life.

TODAY'S AFFIRMATION

I live with joy, filling my life with purpose and peace.

INSTANT POSITIVITY **85**

JAN

FEB

MAR

APR

MAY

JUN

JUL

AUG

SEP

OCT

NOV

DEC

March 12

CELEBRATE YOUR LIFE

"The more you praise and celebrate your life,
the more there is in life to celebrate."

—Oprah Winfrey

Your life is worth celebrating every single day. Every moment you're alive is a testament to the incredible miracle that you are. Think about all the amazing things that had to align for you to come into existence—and all the right (and even wrong) turns that brought you to this very moment. Each day is a gift, filled with opportunities to grow, love, learn, and shine. Embrace the journey that has led you here, and recognize that your story is worth celebrating daily!

TODAY'S ACTION

Please list all the amazing things in your life, and prepare to celebrate them like your birthday! Think big, think small, and get excited about every single one. From significant achievements to simple joys like a warm cup of coffee or a friendly smile, treat each reason as a special gift. Crank up your favorite song, do a little dance, and let yourself feel the joy of these blessings.

TODAY'S AFFIRMATION

I celebrate my life every day.

March 13

CREATE CALM AND CONFIDENCE

"Wisdom is an organized life."

—Immanuel Kant

An organized closet is a secret weapon for calm and confidence. Your space reflects order and intention, bringing a sense of ease and joy to your day. Decluttering isn't just about tidying up; it's about making room for what truly supports and uplifts you. Organize your space into a place of inspiration, not stress, and watch how it elevates your life.

TODAY'S ACTION

Refresh your closet today by removing the clothes you no longer wear. As you hold each item, ask yourself if it adds joy or purpose to your life. Donate what no longer serves you, knowing it will go to someone who truly appreciates it. Feel the lightness and clarity this brings to your life!

TODAY'S AFFIRMATION

I create peace and purpose by letting go of what no longer serves me.

JAN

FEB

MAR

APR

MAY

JUN

JUL

AUG

SEP

OCT

NOV

DEC

March 14

ACHIEVE AGAINST ALL ODDS

"Mirror, mirror on the wall, I'll always get up after I fall. And whether I run, walk, or have to crawl, I'll set my goals and achieve them all."

—CHRIS BUTLER

True strength lies in your unwavering commitment to your dreams. Challenges may slow you down, but they don't define your path. Each step, whether big or small, brings you closer to your goals. When you choose persistence over doubt, you unlock a reservoir of resilience, proving that no challenge can keep you from reaching what you set your heart on. Success isn't about the pace—it's about the persistence.

TODAY'S ACTION

Pick a goal you've felt distant from and take one intentional action. No matter the size of the step, honor it as a commitment to yourself. Remember that progress is progress, whether sprinting, walking or even crawling forward. By doing this, you reaffirm your dedication to yourself, no matter your challenges.

TODAY'S AFFIRMATION

I am unstoppable and achieve my goals with resilience and determination.

March 15

RELEASE AND RISE

"Holding on is believing there's only a past;
letting go is knowing there's a future."

—DAPHNE ROSE KINGMA

Letting go frees you to live fully in the present. Carrying old hurts is like a shadow that follows you and blocks the brightness of your future. Letting go isn't about erasing the past. It's about freeing yourself from pain that no longer serves you. When you release it, you make room for new joy, peace, and growth. Embracing the future with hope is a powerful act of self-love that opens the way for a brighter tomorrow.

TODAY'S ACTION

Today, take a moment to reflect on any hurt you're still carrying from the past. Visualize these feelings as heavy weights you can't put down. Gently tell yourself, "It's time to let this go." Imagine setting down these weights and walking forward feeling lighter, more open, and ready for new possibilities. If it feels right, write down what you're letting go of and then tear up the paper as a symbolic act of release. You could even feel this weight of release by sharing it with someone else.

TODAY'S AFFIRMATION

I let go of the past and open my heart to peace and freedom.

FEB

MAR

APR

MAY

JUN

JUL

AUG

SEP

OCT

NOV

DEC

March 16

BOOST YOURSELF UP

"You become what you envision yourself being."

—Lewis Howes

Self-talk has the power to shape your reality. It's easy to see your flaws and be your own worst critic, but how do you take the time to lift yourself? Be your own best friend. Giving yourself a pep talk can be one of the most potent ways to build confidence, motivation, and resilience. By speaking to yourself with kindness and encouragement, you cultivate self-belief and the strength to overcome any challenge.

TODAY'S ACTION

When was the last time you gave yourself a pep talk? Today, whenever you face a challenge or feel doubt creeping in, choose a phrase that resonates with you, like "I can do this!" or "I am capable and strong." Say it out loud with conviction, and notice how this simple act can shift your mindset from self-doubt to self-assurance. If confidence feels hard to find, remember you're not alone—seek support from those around you or through prayer.

TODAY'S AFFIRMATION

I have the power to uplift and encourage myself every day.

March 17

TAKE A GRATITUDE WALK

"Gratitude can transform common days into thanksgivings, turn routine jobs into joy, and change ordinary opportunities into blessings."

—WILLIAM ARTHUR WARD

Gratitude has the power to elevate even the simplest moments. When you practice gratitude, your brain releases endorphins. These "feel-good" chemicals uplift your mood and bring a sense of well-being. William Arthur Ward's words remind us that gratitude can turn routine tasks into moments of joy. Science supports this: studies show that gratitude stimulates the release of these mood-boosting endorphins, reducing stress and increasing happiness. By acknowledging the blessings around you, you can transform your daily experiences, finding joy and beauty even in the most minor things.

TODAY'S ACTION

Take a 10-minute "Gratitude Walk" today. As you walk, make it a game to spot three things you love—like the blue sky, a friendly wave, or the sound of a slight breeze. Feel your mood lift with each step, and let yourself smile! Treat this walk as a bit of adventure, a fun chance to soak in all the beauty around you and get those endorphins flowing.

TODAY'S AFFIRMATION

I am surrounded by beauty and abundance.

JAN
FEB
MAR
APR
MAY
JUN
JUL
AUG
SEP
OCT
NOV
DEC

March 18

WELCOME CHANGE

"Some people don't like change, but you need to embrace change if the alternative is disaster."

—ELON MUSK

Change isn't about breaking free from your comfort zone but expanding it. Embracing change creates room for growth and allows us to build resilience, one step at a time. When we approach change mindfully, we're strengthening the foundation of our comfort zone, making it a place where we can confidently face whatever comes our way. This steady expansion allows us to grow gracefully and navigate new experiences without feeling overwhelmed.

TODAY'S ACTION

Pick one area where you're ready for a fresh change. Start with a small step—try a new habit, switch up your routine, or learn something unfamiliar. See this as a way to stretch your comfort zone and build adaptability. With each intentional step, you're creating a life that feels secure yet open to growth.

TODAY'S AFFIRMATION

I expand my comfort zone with courage, inviting growth and resilience.

March 19

FLEXIBILITY FOR LIFE

"The best 'hack' for a good day: quiet reflection, sunlight, and stretching."

—Dr. Amy Shah

Flexibility is freedom—it lets you move with ease through life. Stretching isn't just for the body. It's a gift to your mind and soul, too. Keeping your body flexible keeps your energy flowing, helping you feel younger, lighter, and more resilient. Stretching regularly helps reduce tension, boost your mood, and lift your spirit. Each time you stretch, you're nurturing a foundation of health and well-being that supports you daily.

TODAY'S ACTION

Today, take two minutes every few hours to gently stretch and realign your body. Start with a simple stretch or pilates in the morning, focusing on deep breaths and releasing tension. Notice how a small act of flexibility can bring a sense of calm, energy, and clarity to your day.

TODAY'S AFFIRMATION

I honor my body's strength and flexibility.

JAN

FEB

MAR

APR

MAY

JUN

JUL

AUG

SEP

OCT

NOV

DEC

March 20

LEARN THROUGH CURIOSITY

"What you don't know can become your greatest asset if you let it. If you're open to learning and asking questions."

—Sara Blakely

Embracing what you don't know is a gateway to growth. Rather than seeing gaps in knowledge as limitations, view them as opportunities. Curiosity is the foundation for innovation and personal transformation. When you allow yourself to be open and ask questions, you invite fresh insights and creative ideas that lead you closer to your goals.

TODAY'S ACTION

Choose an area in your life or a skill where you feel you lack knowledge. Reach out to someone with expertise in this area, ask questions, or spend time researching it. One actionable step to expand your understanding today is reading an article, listening to a podcast, or trying something hands-on. Every small effort builds your knowledge and strengthens your journey.

TODAY'S AFFIRMATION

I embrace what I don't know and let curiosity guide me to growth.

March 21

CELEBRATE THE SKIN YOU'RE IN

"I've made peace with the fact that the things I thought were weaknesses or flaws were just me. I like them."

—Sandra Bullock

True self-acceptance means embracing your so-called flaws. Self-acceptance is about embracing the unique qualities that make you who you are. The imperfections you once saw are simply parts of your individuality and strength. You see beauty in your authenticity when you make peace with these features. Let today be a reminder that absolute confidence comes from valuing every part of yourself exactly as you are.

TODAY'S ACTION

Every time you look in the mirror today, take a moment to appreciate your skin. Thank it for everything it does to protect and care for you. Show it some love by moisturizing, enjoying a gentle massage, or simply taking a few quiet moments to pamper it. Give your skin the care it deserves, and let this simple act shift your perspective to self-love and acceptance.

TODAY'S AFFIRMATION

I am grateful for the skin I'm in.

JAN

FEB

MAR

APR

MAY

JUN

JUL

AUG

SEP

OCT

NOV

DEC

March 22

HIKE TO HAPPINESS

"To walk in nature is to witness a thousand miracles."

—MARY DAVIS

Nothing recharges you like time in nature. Hiking offers an incredible blend of movement and peace, helping you feel alive and connected. Each step on a trail strengthens your heart, builds your muscles, and calms your mind. Studies show that even a short walk outdoors lowers stress, boosts mood, and fills you with energy. Hiking is more than exercise—it's a path to joy and inner calm.

TODAY'S ACTION

Plan a hike today that allows you to immerse yourself in nature. Whether it's your neighborhood, a local trail, or a more adventurous path, let yourself enjoy every part of the experience. Breathe deeply and listen to the sounds around you. Let nature refresh your mind and body.

TODAY'S AFFIRMATION

Nature allows me to feel recharged, peaceful, and positive.

March 23

SHOW UP FOR YOURSELF

"No matter how you feel, get up, dress up,
and show up for your dreams."

—REGINA BRETT

Showing up for yourself is an act of self-respect.
When you prioritize what brings you joy, you create
happiness and honor your purpose. Whenever you
choose to engage in what you love, you build resilience,
lift your spirit, and show the world—and yourself—that
your dreams matter. This commitment, showing up for
yourself, makes life feel more positive and meaningful.

TODAY'S ACTION

Follow through on one commitment you've made to
yourself, even if you don't feel like it today. Choose
something that will make a positive difference,
whether a small task or a personal goal. Honoring your
commitments builds grit, strengthens confidence, and
moves you closer to success. Let this act of showing
up remind you of your dedication to yourself and
your dreams.

TODAY'S AFFIRMATION

I honor my commitments and show up for myself
every day.

JAN

FEB

MAR

APR

MAY

JUN

JUL

AUG

SEP

OCT

NOV

DEC

March 24

FILL YOUR SPIRIT

"Man has two great spiritual needs. One is for forgiveness.
The other is for goodness."

—BILLY GRAHAM

Forgiveness and goodness are gifts that enrich the soul.
Forgiveness frees us from the weight of past hurts, while
goodness fills our hearts with compassion, purpose, and
light. Embracing both allows us to move forward with
peace and grace, healing ourselves and others. When we
seek forgiveness and pursue goodness, we align with our
highest potential and create a life of true growth.

TODAY'S ACTION

Reflect on one area where you can offer forgiveness—to
yourself or someone else. Then, identify a small act of
goodness you can bring into today's world. This action
could be a kind word, a thoughtful gesture, or a few
minutes dedicated to helping someone in need. Embrace
these two acts as a reminder of your power to bring
peace and positivity into your life.

TODAY'S AFFIRMATION

I uplift my spirit by choosing forgiveness and goodness.

March 25

EXPAND YOUR COMFORT ZONE

"The Comfort Zone is not a static place. If we allow it, our Comfort Zone will continually grow and expand. It is always becoming more."

—KRISTEN BUTLER

Expansion is the purpose of this life. Your growth is shaped by the "Zone of Living" where you spend the most time: the comfort zone, the survival zone, or the complacent zone. Many people are encouraged to consistently step outside their Comfort Zone, pushing them into the Survival or Complacent Zone, where stress and overwhelm take over. Real, lasting growth happens when you stop shaming yourself for your comfort zone and learn how to expand it—where you feel safe, supported, and empowered.

TODAY'S ACTION

Reflect on which zone you tend to spend the most time in. Are you spending too much time in the Survival Zone, or have you settled into the Complacent Zone? Type in your browser comfortzonequiz.com to help identify your zone. Commit to small steps that expand your Comfort Zone, achieving growth in a sustainable and positive way.

TODAY'S AFFIRMATION

I easily expand my comfort zone, creating a life of growth and fulfillment.

JAN

FEB

MAR

APR

MAY

JUN

JUL

AUG

SEP

OCT

NOV

DEC

March 26

REST WITH INTENTION

"Tired minds don't plan well. Sleep first, plan later."

—WALTER REISCH

Good sleep is the foundation of a healthy, focused mind.
Quality rest supports your body's essential functions,
from boosting cognitive clarity and emotional resilience
to strengthening your immune system. Without it, even
the simplest tasks feel harder, and stress creeps in. Sleep
isn't just a luxury—it's a vital part of your journey to well-
being, success, and positivity.

TODAY'S ACTION

Tonight, create a calming bedtime routine. Start by
limiting screen time and blue light exposure an hour
before bed. Dim the lights, light a candle, and enjoy a
book or some journaling to wind down. Let these small
steps signal to your mind and body that it's time to rest,
helping you sleep peacefully and wake up refreshed.

TODAY'S AFFIRMATION

I am intentional about creating restful sleep habits that
support my well-being.

March 27

WALK IN THE SUNSHINE

"Keep your face always toward the sunshine—
and shadows will fall behind you."

—WALT WHITMAN

When you focus on the light, everything changes.
Positivity is a choice that fills your life with sunshine, lifting
you above challenges and letting joy lead the way. Like
sunlight, positive energy illuminates what's beautiful,
creating a ripple effect of gratitude and resilience.
Embrace the habit of turning toward the sunshine and let
the shadows fall behind you.

TODAY'S ACTION

Take a "Positivity Walk" today! Step outside or walk
around your space, and focus solely on the positives
in your life. With each step, think of something you're
grateful for, a recent accomplishment, or a small joy. Let
this walk be a celebration of all the good in your life, and
feel your energy shift.

TODAY'S AFFIRMATION

I focus on the light, creating a life of joy and resilience.

March 28

BUILD JOYFUL CONNECTIONS

"Alone we can do so little; together we can do so much."

—HELEN KELLER

Connection is the heartbeat of a joyful life. So much of our happiness comes from the moments we share with others. We're not meant to go through life alone. A single conversation with someone who fills your cup can leave you feeling uplifted and energized for days. Meaningful connections reduce stress, boost well-being, and remind us of the beauty of shared experiences. Whether it's a quick call or a heartfelt conversation, reaching out can light up your day and theirs, creating a ripple of positivity and growth that lasts long after the interaction.

TODAY'S ACTION

Plan a "connection moment" today. Choose someone you miss and set up a quick video call or send them a voice note instead of a regular text. Please share a favorite memory you have with them or ask about a recent win in their life. This slight, personal touch shows you care and opens the door for a more meaningful conversation.

TODAY'S AFFIRMATION

I am surrounded by relationships that uplift and support me.

March 29

ALIGN WITH THE PRESENT

"Yesterday is history, tomorrow is a mystery, today is a gift of God, which is why we call it the present."

—BIL KEANE

The power of today lies in your presence. It's a gift to be fully present. When you embrace this moment, you let go of the past and release worries about the future. Being here now connects you to peace, purpose, possibility, and positivity. Each moment invites you to savor life's abundance, grounding you in the beauty of what's genuine.

TODAY'S ACTION

As you prepare for bed tonight, slow down and savor each slight movement. Be fully present in every action— whether brushing your teeth, tidying up, or simply walking. Feel the ground beneath your feet, the rhythm of your breath, and the gentle flow of your muscles. Each time your mind wanders, gently return to the moment. Let this quiet practice bring you into harmony with yourself, inviting curiosity, acceptance, and calm into your evening.

TODAY'S AFFIRMATION

I am here now, fully present in each moment.

JAN

FEB

MAR

APR

MAY

JUN

JUL

AUG

SEP

OCT

NOV

DEC

March 30

FIND PEACE IN STILLNESS

"We need to find God, and he cannot be found in noise and restlessness. God is the friend of silence."

—MOTHER TERESA

Silence creates space for connection, clarity, and inner peace. In a world filled with constant noise and distraction, embracing silence allows us to tune into our deepest thoughts and God's presence. By stepping away from the noise, we open ourselves to peace, strength, and guidance found only in stillness.

TODAY'S ACTION

Invite moments of silence into your day, even if it's only a few minutes at a time. Turn off any background noise, close your eyes, and sit quietly. Notice how the silence feels—does it bring calm, restlessness, or something in between? Take a deep breath. Observe without judgment, allowing the stillness to settle within you. Let this practice draw you closer to inner peace within yourself and God.

TODAY'S AFFIRMATION

In silence, I find strength, peace, and connection.

March 31

EMBRACE DARK MOMENTS

"Only in the darkness can you see the stars."

—MARTIN LUTHER KING JR.

In the dark, we learn to seek the light. Challenges, like darkness, hold the seeds of growth and resilience. When we face difficult times, we're given a chance to build strength, faith, and a deeper appreciation for life's light. Embracing dark moments doesn't mean giving in to them. It means allowing them to shape us into wiser, more resilient people. Just as the dawn feels brightest after the night, we discover our capacity for joy and purpose through our struggles.

TODAY'S ACTION

Today, reflect on a challenge you're facing or have faced recently. Take a few minutes to journal how this challenge could be helping you grow or see life in a new way. What insights or strengths has it revealed within you? Embrace this perspective, allowing yourself to feel gratitude for the growth that hardship brings.

TODAY'S AFFIRMATION

Through every challenge, I find strength, light, and growth.

April

LIVE YOUR MASTERPIECE

"Every human is an artist. The dream of your life is to make beautiful art."

—Don Miguel Ruiz

Your life is a canvas—paint it with purpose. Every choice, thought, and dream is a brushstroke on the canvas of your life. When you see yourself as an artist, you begin to live with intention, creativity, and meaning. This approach invites you to shape a life that's your own —creating one that expresses who you are.

TODAY'S ACTION

Today, actively bring creativity into your life. Choose one small activity that lets you express yourself—doodling, writing a short poem or article, creating social media content, rearranging a room, or cooking a unique meal. Let this be a reminder that every action can be infused with creativity. Capture the experience with a photo to create a memory you may want to reflect on later.

TODAY'S AFFIRMATION

I am the artist of my life, creating with purpose and vision.

JAN
FEB
MAR
APR
MAY
JUN
JUL
AUG
SEP
OCT
NOV
DEC

April 2

SET GOALS THAT INSPIRE YOU

"A goal should scare you a little and excite you a lot."

—DR. JOE VITALE

Goals are the bridge between your dreams and reality.
A decisive goal doesn't just motivate you—it lights you up
and gives you a reason to move forward with purpose.
Setting SMART goals brings clarity and structure to your
vision, creating a specific, measurable, achievable,
relevant, and time-bound path. SMART goals make your
dreams feel real and within reach, one step at a time.

TODAY'S ACTION

Create a "SMART Spark" goal. Reflect on this week's
insights, focusing on one meaningful goal that excites
and challenges you. Write down your SMART goal, and
add one small, simple step you can take today to move
closer to it. Keep this goal visible and let it fuel your
momentum each day.

TODAY'S AFFIRMATION

I am dedicated to my growth, turning dreams into reality
with clear and inspiring goals.

April 3

HEAR WITH YOUR HEART

"The most basic of all human needs is the need to understand and be understood. The best way to understand people is to listen to them."

—RALPH NICHOLS

Listening is love in action. In a world of constant noise, genuinely listening is a rare gift. When we listen with our hearts, we honor the speaker's thoughts and emotions, creating a space where they feel seen and valued. This intentional act deepens empathy and trust and builds a powerful connection. A few moments of genuine, undivided attention can open doors to deeper understanding and bring warmth into our relationships.

TODAY'S ACTION

Create a "Listening Moment" today. Choose someone—a friend, neighbor, coworker, or family member—and ask them a simple question like, "How's your day going?" or "What's on your mind?" Listen with patience, without interrupting or planning your response. Notice how focusing on them, even for a few minutes, creates connection and warmth. If in-person isn't possible, give your full, genuine attention over the phone or in a text.

TODAY'S AFFIRMATION

I listen with love and an open heart.

JAN
FEB
MAR
APR
MAY
JUN
JUL
AUG
SEP
OCT
NOV
DEC

April 4

OWN YOUR TRUTH

"You can't change what you don't acknowledge."

—Dr. Phil

Real transformation begins with honesty. Facing the truths within ourselves—whether they're old habits, limiting beliefs, or uncomfortable emotions—opens the door to change. When you allow awareness, you reclaim your power to grow and evolve. You allow yourself to let go of what doesn't serve you. This first step may feel challenging, but it's the key to building a life rooted in authenticity, purpose, and positivity.

TODAY'S ACTION

Choose one area where you've felt resistance or know change is needed. Take a quiet moment to acknowledge it fully by speaking it aloud or sharing it with someone you trust. Then, set an intention for how you want this part of your life to evolve—letting go of a habit, shifting your mindset, or inviting new energy. This action step is a loving commitment to yourself. Every step forward brings you closer to transformation.

TODAY'S AFFIRMATION

I am brave enough to face my truth and create positive change.

April 5

DEEPEN YOUR CONNECTION

"Eye contact is way more intimate than words can ever be."

—FARAAZ KAZI

A simple gaze can unlock a world of connection. Eye contact goes beyond words, creating a bridge between souls. It's no wonder it can feel both vulnerable and powerful. Looking into your partner's eyes brings a level of closeness that words cannot reach. This shared moment allows you to see and be seen more deeply, strengthening trust, affection, and understanding.

TODAY'S ACTION

Set aside a few quiet moments to try eye gazing with your partner today. Sit comfortably facing each other in a peaceful space and softly focus on each other's eyes without speaking. Allow any initial discomfort to pass and feel the warmth and love grow in the silence. If you're single, try a similar practice with yourself in the mirror to connect deeply with your essence.

TODAY'S AFFIRMATION

I have meaningful connections that deepen my love and understanding.

JAN

FEB

MAR

APR

MAY

JUN

JUL

AUG

SEP

OCT

NOV

DEC

April 6

CHOOSE WITH PURPOSE

"Clutter is nothing more than postponed decisions."

—Barbara Hemphill

Clutter is a silent weight we carry. When we put off decisions, we allow distractions to accumulate in our spaces and lives. Letting go of what doesn't serve us is an act of freedom, clearing a path for choices that reflect our true intentions. Embracing this clarity creates space for energy, positivity, and purpose to thrive. When we make decisions purposefully, we create a life filled with positivity.

TODAY'S ACTION

Take 20 minutes today to clean and organize your fridge with purpose. Remove foods that make you feel shame or regret, wipe down shelves, and toss expired or unhelpful items. Arrange healthier options at eye level, making it easy to reach for foods that fuel you. Group similar items together for easy access. Notice how this simple act of organization leaves you feeling lighter and more energized.

TODAY'S AFFIRMATION

Every choice nourishes my body and brings me closer to my best self.

April 7

CONNECT WITH THE EARTH

"Every step you take is different when you're barefoot."

—Michael Franti

Walking barefoot brings us closer to nature's rhythm.
When your feet connect directly with the Earth, you
become present with each step, releasing stress and
welcoming calm. This simple act is backed by science,
grounds your energy, reduces stress, and renews your
connection with the world. You'll find peace, clarity, and a
fresh perspective in each barefoot step.

TODAY'S ACTION

Find a safe patch of grass and take a few minutes to
walk barefoot during a break today. Focus on the feel of
the grass beneath you—cool, soft, and grounding. Slow
your breathing, release tension, and imagine the Earth's
calming energy flowing through your feet. This small
act reconnects you with nature, leaving you refreshed
and centered. Do this anytime your energy feels
compromised.

TODAY'S AFFIRMATION

I am grounded, calm, and connected to the Earth.

JAN
FEB
MAR
APR
MAY
JUN
JUL
AUG
SEP
OCT
NOV
DEC

April 8

MAKE ROOM FOR LAUGHTER

"I believe that laughing is the best calorie burner."

—DREW BARRYMORE

Laughter truly is the ultimate "calorie burner" for the soul! It lightens your heart, eases your mind, and gives your spirit a little workout. Choosing joy and finding reasons to laugh—even when things get tough—keeps you strong, resilient, and full of positive energy. As Drew reminds us, laughter is a gift that lifts our spirits and strengthens us from the inside out.

TODAY'S ACTION

Brighten your day by watching some funny videos! Pull up your favorite stand-up comedy, a hilarious skit, or short videos that make you laugh. As you take breaks today, dive into the joy of laughter and let it lift your mood. Notice how each laugh makes you feel lighter and more connected to the present moment. Let yourself laugh generously, and feel how it brings calm, energy, and positivity into your day.

TODAY'S AFFIRMATION

I make space for laughter and joy every day.

April 9

SURF THE WAVES OF EMOTION

"Feelings are like waves; we can't stop them,
but we can choose which one to surf."

—JONATAN MÅRTENSSON

Emotions rise and fall, but your response is your power.
You can turn anxiety into calm by choosing which
"wave" to ride. Simple actions that release serotonin and
endorphins—your body's natural mood boosters—can
bring peace and positivity into your day.

TODAY'S ACTION

Boost your serotonin and endorphins with a tiny action
today. Take a quick walk outside, enjoy a few minutes of
sunshine, or watch a funny video to lighten your mood.
Add a food high in tryptophan, like a banana, to your
snack for an extra serotonin boost. Small choices like
these add up, helping you manage stress naturally while
uplifting your spirit.

TODAY'S AFFIRMATION

I choose peace and positivity in every moment.

JAN

FEB

MAR

APR

MAY

JUN

JUL

AUG

SEP

OCT

NOV

DEC

April 10

BELIEVE IN YOUR WORTH

"The world sees your value when you believe in it first."

—Lewis Howes

Positivity and self-worth are deeply connected. When you recognize your worth, you naturally attract more positive experiences and relationships into your life. Studies show that self-compassion and self-acceptance lead to greater resilience and overall well-being, creating a foundation for positivity that radiates outward. Believing in your worth isn't just about confidence—it's about giving yourself permission to live with positivity and purpose.

TODAY'S ACTION

Take a "Worth Pause" today. Find a quiet moment to close your eyes, take a deep breath, and reflect on one quality you love about yourself. Please write it down or say it out loud, allowing yourself to truly feel its importance. Write "I am enough" on a sticky note and place it on your bathroom mirror for extra credit. Pause each time you see it and remind yourself of your innate value.

TODAY'S AFFIRMATION

I believe in my worth and prioritize positivity.

April 11

FOCUS BRINGS SUCCESS

"The successful warrior is the average man, with laser-like focus."

—BRUCE LEE

True power comes from where you place your focus.
Success isn't about doing everything but choosing what
truly matters. Like a warrior in training, channeling your
energy toward a single purpose turns ordinary moments
into extraordinary progress. By directing your focus, you
actively shape your life to reflect your deepest goals
and dreams. Every small, intentional action adds up to
significant results.

TODAY'S ACTION

Find success by creating a "Focus Zone" for one critical
task. Take 10 minutes to remove all distractions from
your space—turn off notifications, close unrelated tabs,
or use noise-canceling headphones. Set a timer for
30–60 minutes and dive into your task with full attention.
Feel the power of uninterrupted focus and enjoy the
satisfaction of making real progress.

TODAY'S AFFIRMATION

I focus intently on what brings me closer to my goals.

April 12

PROGRESS OVER PERFECTION

"Don't let the perfect be the enemy of the good."

—Voltaire

Perfection isn't the goal—progress is. Your inner critic can cloud your mind with doubts, convincing you that "good" isn't enough. But here's the truth: your worth isn't defined by perfection. Learning to silence that inner critic opens the door to self-compassion and a more transparent, optimistic view of yourself. When you quiet that voice, you make room for growth, joy, and authentic self-acceptance.

TODAY'S ACTION

Give your inner critic the day off. When it chimes in with negativity, imagine locking it away and saying aloud, "I choose to focus on my strengths and growth today." Replace critical thoughts with something you're proud of or a positive quality you're developing. This slight shift can make a powerful difference, reminding you that you're progressing.

TODAY'S AFFIRMATION

I celebrate my progress and take another step forward.

April 13

UNPLUG TO RECHARGE

"Sometimes you have to unplug yourself from the world for a moment so that you can reset yourself."

—Vex King

Stepping away is a powerful way to recharge. In our fast-paced world, intentional pauses allow us to reset, gain perspective, and find the positivity within us. Research shows that even short moments of unplugging can reduce stress, improve focus, and boost emotional resilience. By unplugging, you're giving yourself space to breathe, reset, and return stronger.

TODAY'S ACTION

Plan a "Sunrise Reset" this week! Pick a day to wake up early, find a peaceful spot—a nearby park, backyard, or a local viewpoint—and watch the sunrise. Bring a warm drink, a blanket, and a journal. As the sun rises, take a few deep breaths, soak in the stillness, and let go of any lingering stress. You can even post a photo and tag me! Use this quiet time to write down three things you're grateful for and set a positive intention for your day.

TODAY'S AFFIRMATION

I unplug to recharge, finding peace in moments of quiet.

JAN
FEB
MAR
APR
MAY
JUN
JUL
AUG
SEP
OCT
NOV
DEC

April 14

POWER IN PRIORITIES

"Do the hard jobs first. The easy jobs will take care of themselves."

—DALE CARNEGIE

The most complex tasks hold the most power. When we avoid what feels difficult, it lingers in our minds, draining energy and focus. Facing it head-on can release a sense of relief and accomplishment, opening up space for progress. Tackle the tough stuff first, and watch how it transforms your day, leaving you lighter and more confident.

TODAY'S ACTION

Identify the task or project that's been weighing on you. Break it down into simple, manageable steps, and focus on the next one. Aim to complete that step today, no matter how small. Every bit of progress builds momentum, and tackling what feels hardest instantly boosts your confidence.

TODAY'S AFFIRMATION

I focus on priorities that lead to my success.

April 15

DEEPEN YOUR BREATH

"Just breathe. You are strong enough to handle your challenges."

—LORI DESCHENE

Your breath is your anchor. Deep breathing does more than calm your mind—it empowers you to overcome life's challenges with strength. Research shows deep breathing activates the parasympathetic nervous system, reducing stress hormones and enhancing focus and resilience. When anxious, breathing deprives your brain of essential oxygen, which can cloud your judgment. By breathing deeply, you give yourself the energy and calm to face whatever comes your way.

TODAY'S ACTION

Practice taking three deep breaths every hour today. Inhale slowly through your nose, filling your lungs, then exhale through your mouth and release any tension. Notice how each breath centers you, enhances focus, and refreshes your energy.

TODAY'S AFFIRMATION

I breathe in calm and exhale all the tension.

JAN
FEB
MAR
APR
MAY
JUN
JUL
AUG
SEP
OCT
NOV
DEC

April 16

OWN THE DAY

"The moment you take responsibility for everything in your life is the moment you can change anything in your life."

—HAL ELROD

How you start each morning shapes your entire day.
When you embrace a morning routine that uplifts and centers you, you create a strong foundation for the hours ahead. By taking ownership of the first moments of your day, you set a positive tone that carries you through challenges and enhances your focus, energy, and well-being. Each morning is a new opportunity to create the life you want.

TODAY'S ACTION

Design a simple morning routine that energizes and inspires you. It might include a few minutes of quiet reflection, setting an intention for the day, light movement, or reading something positive. Start with one or two activities you love and commit to doing them daily. Notice how this practice shapes your mood, mindset, and productivity. To supercharge your morning routine, download our free guide at riseandshineon.com.

TODAY'S AFFIRMATION

I begin each day purposefully, setting the tone for positivity and growth.

April 17

MANIFEST WITH CLARITY

"When I dream and visualize, I'm manifesting powerfully and can see clearly what I want and why I am here."

—CLIONA O'HARA

Visualization is the first step toward turning dreams into reality. When you take time to dream, you connect with your true purpose, building a clear vision of what you want and why it matters. This clarity fuels your focus and strengthens your ability to manifest a life aligned with your values and goals. Every vision, no matter how big or small, begins with a clear mental picture, bringing you closer to the life you're here to live.

TODAY'S ACTION

Create a "Vision Moment." Close your eyes, use your beautiful, creative mind, and imagine yourself confidently living your ideal life, fully aligned with your purpose. Get specific. Picture the details, feel the energy, and connect deeply with this future you. Write down a few words that capture the essence of this vision, and keep them close as a powerful reminder of the path you're creating.

TODAY'S AFFIRMATION

My dreams are clear, and I'm manifesting them with purpose and power.

JAN

FEB

MAR

APR

MAY

JUN

JUL

AUG

SEP

OCT

NOV

DEC

April 18

ALIGN WITH YOUR AUTHENTIC SELF

"The most powerful relationship you will ever have is the relationship with yourself."

—STEVE MARABOLI

Your strongest foundation is the relationship you build with yourself. When you lean inward and align with your true self, you create a life of purpose and self-worth. This connection isn't about isolation but building a foundation of self-trust. When you honor this inner relationship, every choice you make resonates with your values and lifts your spirit.

TODAY'S ACTION

Take some quiet time today to connect inward. Reflect on areas where you need encouragement, direction, or support, and write down one meaningful choice you can make that aligns with who you are and who you wish to become. Whether setting a boundary, taking action toward a goal, or simply showing yourself kindness, commit to this choice as an act of self-trust and self-worth.

TODAY'S AFFIRMATION

I honor who I truly am and embrace my journey.

April 19

ATTRACT POSITIVITY

"The soul attracts that which it secretly harbors;
that which it loves and that which it fears."

—JAMES ALLEN

You are a magnet, drawing in what you hold most deeply. If you fill your inner world with love, hope, and beauty, you'll naturally attract these into your life. But when we allow fear or negativity to linger, we unintentionally invite more of the same. Guard your heart by focusing on what uplifts and inspires you, and let go of anything that doesn't align with the life you want to create. This practice invites beauty, peace, and purpose into every corner of your world.

TODAY'S ACTION

Today, take a few minutes to identify one fear or worry that has been taking up space in your mind. Please write it down, then release it by tearing up the paper or discarding it as a way of letting go. Write down something positive you want to attract—something beautiful or inspiring. Keep this note in a special place as a daily reminder of your intention to welcome positivity.

TODAY'S AFFIRMATION

I guard my heart and attract love, peace, and positivity.

JAN

FEB

MAR

APR

MAY

JUN

JUL

AUG

SEP

OCT

NOV

DEC

April 20

ENVISION YOUR IDEAL LIFE

"Your vision is your compass; let it guide you toward your dreams and aspirations."

—TORY ARCHBOLD

Your vision shapes your reality. Someone once imagined everything that exists. When you realize this, you understand that anything you desire can be achieved if you create it in your mind first. Think about something you've already brought into your life—at one point, it was only a thought. By nurturing it with focus and imagination, you bring it into existence.

TODAY'S ACTION

Create a "Vision Snapshot." Find a quiet space, close your eyes, and imagine a powerful moment from your dream life. Make it as vivid as possible—feel the emotions, hear the sounds, and see the details. Open your eyes and write down this vision snapshot in a sentence or two, capturing the essence of that moment. Keep it somewhere visible to remind you of that next level of your life every day.

TODAY'S AFFIRMATION

I nurture my vision and believe my dreams are possible.

April 21

REACH OUT AND RECONNECT

"Two things you will never have to chase:
true friends and true love."

—MANDY HALE

Genuine connection is a treasure worth nurturing. In the rush of daily life, it's easy to let time slip by without connecting with those who matter most. But hearing a friend's voice, sharing a laugh, or simply letting them know they're in your thoughts is profoundly comforting. Even with a simple call, reconnecting can make a world of difference for them and you. Authentic connections don't need to be chased; they need to be nurtured. By reaching out, you keep these precious bonds alive and strong.

TODAY'S ACTION

Pick up the phone and call a friend you have not spoken to but who's been on your mind. Ask how they're doing, share a memory, or listen. This small connection can brighten both of your days and remind you of the simple joy found in true friendship.

TODAY'S AFFIRMATION

I nurture love and connection through my actions.

JAN
FEB
MAR
APR
MAY
JUN
JUL
AUG
SEP
OCT
NOV
DEC

April 22

SHARE YOUR LIGHT

"Dream big, work hard, stay focused, and surround yourself with positive people who uplift you."

—RICK ORNELAS

The people you allow into your life shape who you become. Positive connections fuel your dreams and keep you focused. You expand your potential when you surround yourself with uplifting and inspiring people. Sharing your light with others invites them to grow with you.

TODAY'S ACTION

Curate your social media to be a positive space. Unfollow any accounts that trigger stress or self-doubt and replace them with those that uplift and inspire you. Follow positive communities, such as Power of Positivity, or authors featured in this book, like Rick Ornelas, to receive daily reminders that support your journey and keep you focused on growth.

TODAY'S AFFIRMATION

I choose to surround myself with positivity and growth-minded people.

April 23

LISTEN WITH PRESENCE

"Listening is about being present, not just about being quiet."

—Krista Tippett

Listening is a powerful act of presence. Listening allows others to feel seen, heard, and valued. This kind of presence fosters trust, empathy, and authentic connection. It's a powerful act that can transform any relationship, bringing warmth, understanding, and positivity into your life.

TODAY'S ACTION

Practice present listening today. When someone speaks, set everything else aside—your phone, thoughts, and responses—and tune in fully. Let your attention be a bridge of connection. Notice how this focused presence strengthens your bond, creating trust and understanding that words alone can't build.

TODAY'S AFFIRMATION

I listen with focus and presence, creating space for authentic connection.

JAN
FEB
MAR
APR
MAY
JUN
JUL
AUG
SEP
OCT
NOV
DEC

April 24

PRESENCE FUELS BLESSINGS

"Be present in all things and thankful for all things."

—Maya Angelou

Presence and gratitude are deeply connected. When you are truly present, you become more aware of the blessings surrounding you, no matter how small. You appreciate the moment, opening your heart to the depths of gratitude. You find joy in everyday experiences and recognize the abundance in your life. Gratitude anchors you in the now, helping you see the beauty in ordinary moments.

TODAY'S ACTION

Start your gratitude jar today. Find a jar or container to dedicate for this purpose, and add one statement of gratitude each day. Please keep it simple: write down what you're grateful for on small pieces of paper and drop them into the jar. Put it somewhere you will see every day. This action step is how you build a gratitude habit and grow. This practice will help you cultivate presence, positivity, and a deeper appreciation for your life.

TODAY'S AFFIRMATION

The more grateful I feel, the more blessings I see.

April 25

FAIL FORWARD

"Accept your failures as steps towards your achievement."

—David Meltzer

Every failure is a stepping stone. Embracing failure as a natural part of growth helps you build resilience, insight, and confidence. Rather than viewing setbacks as roadblocks, see them as essential detours, guiding you closer to your goals with new wisdom. When you harness the lessons from each misstep, you become unstoppable, transforming every challenge into progress.

TODAY'S ACTION

Identify one "failure" you've experienced recently, big or small. Please take a moment to reflect on the lesson hidden within it. Then, turn this lesson into a simple action step that supports your growth and brings you closer to your goal. Let this step remind you that failure is not the end; it's simply a bridge to your next breakthrough.

TODAY'S AFFIRMATION

I grow stronger and wiser and move forward with every step I take.

JAN

FEB

MAR

APR

MAY

JUN

JUL

AUG

SEP

OCT

NOV

DEC

April 26

EMBRACE YOUR CRAZY IDEAS

"Good ideas are always crazy until they're not."

—Elon Musk

Dare to dream the impossible and work toward it every day. Greatness starts with an idea that feels just out of reach. Many world-changing ideas seemed "crazy" until someone believed in them enough to bring them to life. Allowing yourself to dream without limits opens new possibilities, creativity, and growth. Trusting in your ideas, no matter how unconventional, fuels positivity and balance by keeping your passion alive while grounding you in purpose.

TODAY'S ACTION

Identify one "crazy" idea or dream you've had recently, big or small. Please write it down and brainstorm one small step to bring it closer to reality. If your idea feels intimidating, that's okay! Even the boldest dreams start with small, consistent actions. Embrace the excitement of exploring the unknown—this journey fuels your energy and sparks inspiration.

TODAY'S AFFIRMATION

I take action on my big ideas with courage and curiosity.

April 27

ELEVATE YOUR INNER CIRCLE

"Surround yourself with people who illuminate your path."

—KRISTEN BUTLER

Your relationships are a reflection of your aspirations and values. The people closest to you can uplift and inspire or hold you back. Choosing to surround yourself with those who encourage growth, positivity, and purpose strengthens your journey and guides you to live your best life. When you intentionally align with people who believe in your vision and illuminate your path, you create an environment where everyone rises together.

TODAY'S ACTION

Start the "Connection Challenge" today. Reflect on your closest connections and consider how they influence your life. Which relationships bring you energy, inspiration, and alignment with your goals? Choose to spend more time with those who uplift and encourage you, and gracefully create distance from connections that don't reflect the life you're building.

TODAY'S AFFIRMATION

I attract and nurture relationships that uplift and inspire me.

JAN

FEB

MAR

APR

MAY

JUN

JUL

AUG

SEP

OCT

NOV

DEC

April 28

FIND PURPOSE IN PASSION

"The more you lose yourself in something bigger
than yourself, the more energy you will have."

—Norman Vincent Peale

**Positive energy ignites when you're part of something
bigger than yourself.** Dedicating yourself to a purpose
beyond your desires unlocks a powerful source of
positivity and resilience. Embracing a passion that serves
a greater good brings joy, renews your spirit, and fuels
you forward.

TODAY'S ACTION

Lose yourself in service. Choose one meaningful action
that serves a purpose beyond yourself. Whether it's
helping a friend, supporting a cause, or working on a goal
aligned with your values, give it your full attention. Notice
how focusing on something bigger fills your day with
purpose and positive energy.

TODAY'S AFFIRMATION

I serve a purpose bigger than myself.

April 29

ALIGN YOUR TIME

"The key is not to prioritize what's on your schedule, but to schedule your priorities."

—STEPHEN COVEY

Make your schedule a reflection of what truly matters.
Time is precious. When our days fill with obligations that don't align with what truly matters, we feel overcommitted and drained. By creating space for the activities that recharge and inspire us, we set ourselves up for a life filled with positive energy, clarity, and purpose.

TODAY'S ACTION

Take a fresh look at your schedule with clear focus and strong intentions. For each commitment, ask yourself: Does this serve my goals? Does it align with my vision? Does it fuel my purpose? Let go of anything that drains your energy or holds you back. Every 'no' to what doesn't serve you is a bold 'yes' to what truly matters.

TODAY'S AFFIRMATION

I choose commitments that align with my highest goals.

JAN

FEB

MAR

April 30

LIVE WITH INTENTION

APR

"You have done enough. You are enough.
You are loved more than you know."

—YUNG PUEBLO

MAY

Being intentional with your time is an act of self-respect. Our days slip by on autopilot, filled with tasks that drain our energy without genuinely serving us. Today's quote reminds us that our worth isn't tied to productivity—it's rooted in simply being. Honor this truth and make room for what nourishes you. You'll find greater peace and purpose in every moment by consciously choosing how you spend your time.

JUN

JUL

TODAY'S ACTION

AUG

Take 10 minutes to audit your day. Note where your time goes, which tasks bring you joy or energy, and which ones drain you. Identify one area where you can create more space for activities that align with your goals or bring you peace. Minor adjustments in how you spend your time can lead to lasting changes.

SEP

OCT

TODAY'S AFFIRMATION

I am enough, and I choose to live each moment with intention.

NOV

DEC

May

May 1

CELEBRATE YOUR MOTHER

"Motherhood: All love begins and ends there."

—ROBERT BROWNING

Motherhood is where love begins, and strength is nurtured. Our mothers shape us in many ways, filling our lives with love, wisdom, and resilience. Whether your relationship with your mother has been easy, complex, or somewhere in between, creating a positive connection can bring healing and growth. Embracing this bond brings peace and honors the love and lessons that have guided us forward.

TODAY'S ACTION

Take a moment to honor the bond with your mother. Write a note of gratitude, share a memory, or, if you can, give her a call. If the relationship is complex, reflect on a moment of growth or healing in your journal. Let this action bring a sense of peace and positivity to your connection.

TODAY'S AFFIRMATION

I honor the love, wisdom, and strength passed down through my mother.

JAN

FEB

MAR

APR

MAY

JUN

JUL

AUG

SEP

OCT

NOV

DEC

May 2

WALK IN POSITIVITY

"Keep looking up… that's the secret of life."

—SNOOPY (CHARLES M. SCHULZ)

Looking up transforms your outlook. Choosing positivity isn't just a mood—it's a mindset shift that fuels resilience, gratitude, and joy. Each positive thought and moment of appreciation turns you toward the light. By focusing on what's good, you create a ripple of positivity that brightens your world and inspires those around you.

TODAY'S ACTION

Take a "Positivity Walk" today. For 15 minutes, walk with intention, focusing on what fills you with joy. With each step, think of a recent win, a small joy, or something you're grateful for. Let this walk be a celebration of all the good in your life, and feel your energy lift with each step.

TODAY'S AFFIRMATION

I choose positivity, creating joy with every step forward.

May 3

PRACTICE INNER KINDNESS

"Talk to yourself like you would to someone you love."

—Brené Brown

Self-compassion is a powerful tool for healing and growth. While kindness flows easily toward others, we can struggle to offer it to ourselves. Self-criticism and doubt can become habits, but speaking to yourself with gentleness creates space for peace, resilience, and positivity. Embracing compassion for yourself opens the door to acceptance, learning, and genuine transformation.

TODAY'S ACTION

Reflect on a recent challenge or mistake, and instead of being critical, offer yourself words of comfort and understanding. Remind yourself that you're doing your best and that mistakes are part of the journey. Feel how self-compassion eases tension and lifts your spirit.

TODAY'S AFFIRMATION

I am gentle and compassionate with myself, allowing space for growth and healing.

JAN

FEB

MAR

APR

MAY

JUN

JUL

AUG

SEP

OCT

NOV

DEC

May 4

ENERGIZE WITH MOVEMENT

"Exercise is the single best thing you can do for your brain in terms of mood, memory, and learning."

—Dr. John Ratey

Moving your body has a powerful effect on your mood and mindset. Physical activity releases endorphins, your body's natural "feel-good" chemicals, boosting your spirits and filling you with energy and positivity. Whether it's a quick stretch, a short walk, or a burst of activity, movement creates a ripple effect of wellness throughout both body and mind.

TODAY'S ACTION

Add some early morning movement to your day with short bursts of jumping jacks. Start with ten in the morning, and repeat whenever you need a quick energy lift. Feel the rush of endorphins and notice how a few moments of activity can brighten your mood and sharpen your focus more effectively than a sip of caffeine. To supercharge your morning routine with even more energy, download our free guide at riseandshineon.com.

TODAY'S AFFIRMATION

I fill my day with energizing movement that uplifts my body and mind.

May 5

COMMUNICATE WITH CLARITY

"Honest communication is built on truth and integrity and upon respect of the one for the other."

—Benjamin E. Mays

Clear communication is a powerful act of self-respect.
When you openly share your needs, you affirm your worth and allow others to support you fully. Speaking up creates a space for trust and mutual respect. We hold back, worried about being a burden or feeling our needs don't matter. But those who care about you want to help you thrive—those who love you will respect your boundaries, too.

TODAY'S ACTION

Practice setting a healthy boundary today by clearly expressing one of your needs to someone close to you. Be specific and direct, but keep it warm and open. Invite their feedback and discuss how you can support each other. This exercise reinforces that boundaries aren't borders but pathways to healthier relationships.

TODAY'S AFFIRMATION

I honor my needs and communicate with clarity and confidence.

JAN

FEB

MAR

APR

MAY

JUN

JUL

AUG

SEP

OCT

NOV

DEC

May 6

RISE THROUGH LEARNING

"Those who keep learning will keep rising in life."

—CHARLES MUNGER

Learning is your gateway to growth. Every new skill, insight, or understanding builds on your potential and lifts you closer to your goals. When you embrace curiosity and make learning a lifelong habit, you open doors to opportunities that might remain hidden. By learning something new daily, you invest in your future and empower yourself to rise above any challenge.

TODAY'S ACTION

Choose one thing you'd like to learn or explore today. It could be a skill related to your work, a hobby you've been curious about, or even a quick article on a topic of interest. Dedicate at least 15 minutes to researching or practicing it. Celebrate each small step as a decisive move toward personal growth and success.

TODAY'S AFFIRMATION

I am a lifelong learner, open to growth and new possibilities.

May 7

BUILD STRENGTH THROUGH STRUGGLES

"Strength does not come from winning. Your struggles develop your strengths."

—Brian Covey

True strength is built in moments of challenge. It's the setbacks, the difficult times, and the obstacles that shape who we are. When you face struggles, you gain resilience, courage, and insight, creating an unstoppable foundation. Embracing struggles as a part of growth brings a decisive shift in perspective, turning challenges into stepping stones.

TODAY'S ACTION

Expand your comfort zone. Take on a task today that feels challenging. It could be a difficult conversation, a workout you've been avoiding, or tackling a project you've put off. Move forward with the mindset that each step, no matter how tough, builds your strength and expands your comfort zone. Afterward, acknowledge the strength you gained just by showing up.

TODAY'S AFFIRMATION

I grow stronger with each challenge I face.

JAN
FEB
MAR
APR
MAY
JUN
JUL
AUG
SEP
OCT
NOV
DEC

May 8

CHOOSE TO CHANGE

"You will never change your life until you change something you do daily."

—John Maxwell

Real change starts with a tiny shift. Consistency is the secret ingredient that transforms your habits and, ultimately, your life. Committing to change, even negligible, sets the foundation for a ripple effect that impacts everything around you. Harness the power of daily actions as the key to creating the life you love.

TODAY'S ACTION

Create a "Change Tracker" to support a new daily habit. Write your goal at the top of a page and draw a simple grid or checklist for each day of the week. Every time you complete the habit, check it off and add a quick note about how it felt. In seven days, you'll have a clear visual of your progress. Let this tracker be a reminder of the commitment you're making to your future self.

TODAY'S AFFIRMATION

Each day, I choose actions that lead me closer to my dreams.

May 9

THINK POSITIVE THOUGHTS

"You cannot have a positive life and a negative mind."

—Joyce Meyer

The thoughts you allow in your mind shape your entire life. When you fill your mind with positive, uplifting thoughts, you create a strong foundation for joy, resilience, and hope. Positive thinking isn't just a mindset—it's a choice that strengthens you, empowering you to face life's challenges with purpose and peace.

TODAY'S ACTION

Identify one area where negativity sneaks into your mind. Write down a positive, uplifting thought to replace it, or try telling yourself a new story that turns this negative into a positive. Each time that thought appears today, replace it with your new belief. Notice how this simple shift lifts your spirit and renews your outlook.

TODAY'S AFFIRMATION

I fill my mind with thoughts that uplift and inspire me.

May 10

ENJOY MINDFUL MEALS

"Healthy eating is not just about physical health, but mental and emotional health as well."

—Dr. Uma Naidoo

How you eat is as important as what you eat. Mindful eating means being fully present with each bite. It's slowing down, savoring each flavor, and tuning into your body's hunger and satisfaction cues. When you eat mindfully, you honor the experience of nourishing yourself—enjoying the textures, smells, and tastes and genuinely listening to what your body needs. This simple practice brings awareness to each meal, transforming eating from a routine into a self-care ritual.

TODAY'S ACTION

Choose one meal to eat mindfully. Begin by taking a few deep breaths before you start. Notice the colors, smells, and textures on your plate. Take small bites, chew slowly, and savor each flavor. Check-in with yourself halfway through to see if you feel satisfied. Let this experience remind you how nourishing it is to be fully present and care for yourself.

TODAY'S AFFIRMATION

I eat with intention, fueling my body, mind, and spirit.

May 11

FACE THE CHALLENGE FIRST

"Do the hard jobs first. The easy jobs will take care of themselves."

—DALE CARNEGIE

Starting with the most challenging task builds unstoppable confidence. It isn't just about productivity—it's about self-belief. You're setting a powerful tone when tackling the most challenging part of your day. This act of courage energizes you, boosts your momentum, and makes the rest of your day feel lighter and more manageable. Embracing the tough stuff first allows you to meet the day with a clear mind and an empowered spirit.

TODAY'S ACTION

Choose the most challenging task on your to-do list for tomorrow. Break it down if needed, but commit to finishing it first. You'll feel a deep sense of accomplishment and ease by facing the most challenging part of your day head-on. Notice how this practice shifts your energy and sets a positive rhythm for the rest of your day.

TODAY'S AFFIRMATION

I embrace challenges with courage, turning them into victories.

JAN

FEB

MAR

APR

MAY

JUN

JUL

AUG

SEP

OCT

NOV

DEC

May 12

REFLECT ON YOUR GROWTH

"Your mindset determines your outcome. Choose positivity, choose growth, choose greatness."

—RYAN HARTLEY

Growth becomes more meaningful when you recognize how far you've come. We often look for validation from others, but you have the power to acknowledge and appreciate your progress. Small steps forward add up. Each one is a testament to your resilience and strength. When you take the time to honor your journey, you build the confidence to keep going. Reflecting on your growth is a powerful reminder of your ability to overcome, adapt, and expand.

TODAY'S ACTION

Take a few moments today to reflect on the growth you've experienced recently. Consider personal and professional areas—what challenges have you faced, and what skills have you gained? Celebrate your progress, and recognize how each step has contributed to the person you are today.

TODAY'S AFFIRMATION

I celebrate my growth and honor the person I am becoming.

May 13

REST TO RESET

"If you don't pick a day to rest, your body will pick it for you."

—DR. AMY SHAH

Taking time to pause is powerful. A few minutes of doing nothing can reset your energy and clear your mind, especially when life feels overwhelming. Stepping back may feel counterintuitive, but it helps you release stress, regain focus, and boost productivity. Research shows short breaks throughout the day can lift your mood, reduce burnout, and strengthen focus. Sometimes, doing nothing is exactly what you need to do.

TODAY'S ACTION

After reading this, close the book, take a few deep breaths, and allow yourself to do nothing for five minutes. Notice how you feel afterward, and return to this quick reset whenever needed. By choosing to pause, you're telling yourself: "I trust the process, and everything is falling into place."

TODAY'S AFFIRMATION

I honor my need for rest and renewal.

JAN

FEB

MAR

APR

MAY

JUN

JUL

AUG

SEP

OCT

NOV

DEC

May 14

SEE THE BEAUTY IN GRATITUDE

"The more grateful I am, the more beauty I see."

—MARY DAVIS

Gratitude is a powerful lens that brings more beauty to our world. When we focus on what we're thankful for, we open our eyes to the hidden beauty in everyday moments. Practicing gratitude shifts our mindset, allowing us to see opportunities, connections, and joys we may have overlooked. This positive shift doesn't just improve our outlook; it creates a ripple effect, enriching our lives and the lives of those around us.

TODAY'S ACTION

Start a "Gratitude Snapshot" collage today. Take a moment to pause and notice three things you're grateful for right now. They could be simple—a cup of coffee, peace, or even the sun shining. Write them down in your journal or snap a quick photo of these moments. Revisit these snapshots as a reminder of the good that surrounds you and challenge yourself to do it again. Evening gratitude will help you carry a grateful heart for rest and even into tomorrow.

TODAY'S AFFIRMATION

I am grateful and see beauty all around me.

May 15

BREATHE IN BALANCE

"Essential oils are a simple yet powerful way to support your body, mind, and emotions."

—Dr. Josh Axe

Your environment shapes your energy and mindset.
Essential oils boost your space naturally, helping you feel energized, calm, or focused. Each scent offers unique benefits—bright citrus invigorates your morning, soothing lavender winds down your evening, and grounding frankincense enhances mindfulness and meditation. Aromatherapy isn't just about fragrance; it's a way to bring nature's nurturing touch to your physical and mental well-being.

TODAY'S ACTION

Explore essential oils that resonate with your needs. Research their benefits, or visit a local store to sample a few scents. Choose a high-quality oil, add a few drops to your diffuser with distilled water, and let the aroma transform your space into a sanctuary of calm.

TODAY'S AFFIRMATION

I create a nurturing space that supports my well-being.

JAN

FEB

MAR

APR

MAY

JUN

JUL

AUG

SEP

OCT

NOV

DEC

May 16

EMBRACE YOUR INNER CHILD

"The most sophisticated people I know - inside,
they are all children."

—JIM HENSON

Within us all lives a child, still longing for love, joy, and healing. This "inner child" carries the unhealed wounds and the pure joy of our past. Reconnecting with this part of ourselves is more than a trip down memory lane—it's a powerful way to heal, grow, and bring lightness back into our lives. By nurturing your child within, you acknowledge the parts of yourself that still need love and acceptance, allowing yourself to feel whole and resilient.

TODAY'S ACTION

Find a peaceful moment to breathe and connect with your inner child. Imagine speaking to them gently, offering words of kindness and reassurance. You can even write a letter expressing love, acceptance, and safety to this younger part of yourself. For a touch of fun, indulge in something your childhood self loved—like drawing, playing a favorite song, or visiting a spot that holds happy memories. Embracing your inner child infuses your life with healing, joy, and a renewed sense of wonder.

TODAY'S AFFIRMATION

I nurture my inner child with love, joy, and acceptance.

May 17

LET CONFIDENCE BE YOUR LIGHT

"The science of charisma shows that confidence is not just how you feel, but how you make others feel."

—Vanessa Van Edwards

True confidence begins within. It's grounded in knowing your worth, trusting your instincts, and embracing yourself. When you're confident from the inside out, you don't just lift yourself—you lift everyone around you. Your energy sends a message of self-assurance that invites others to believe in themselves, too. Confidence is contagious, creating a ripple of empowerment wherever you go.

TODAY'S ACTION

As you go through your day, consciously embody confidence. How would the most confident version of you dress, stand, speak, and interact? Create opportunities to feel good about yourself and extend that uplifting energy to others. Notice how your confidence inspires the people around you.

TODAY'S AFFIRMATION

I radiate confidence, uplifting and inspiring others.

JAN

FEB

MAR

APR

MAY

JUN

JUL

AUG

SEP

OCT

NOV

DEC

May 18

THINK LESS, DO MORE

"Overthinking is like a rocking chair. It gives you
something to do but doesn't get you anywhere."

—GLENN TURNER

Nothing good comes from overthinking. Overthinking
creates a loop that drains our energy without moving us
forward. When we get lost in endless thoughts, it clouds
our clarity and blocks our ability to act. Replacing this
habit with purposeful action brings us closer to our goals
and clears the path to a positive, fulfilling life. Sometimes,
the best way to see things is to step back, breathe,
and begin.

TODAY'S ACTION

Notice when you start to overthink today and take a
single, purposeful action instead. Choose one small step,
however simple, to move forward. The key is breaking the
cycle of endless thoughts by acting and trusting each
small move that brings you closer to your vision.

TODAY'S AFFIRMATION

I foster a positive mindset and take positive action
towards my vision.

May 19

GREATNESS IS A CHOICE

"Greatness isn't something you're born with;
it's something you choose every day."

—LEWIS HOWES

True greatness is about consistently showing up. Even on the most challenging days, you give it your best and choose to grow. Embracing your potential means recognizing that each small action brings you closer to who you're meant to be. Studies show that setting intentional daily goals and practicing self-discipline can significantly improve motivation and overall life satisfaction. Every step forward, no matter how small, is a powerful choice in building your best self.

TODAY'S ACTION

Start your day by setting a "Greatness Goal"—a small, achievable step that aligns with your dreams and pushes you 1% closer. Whether completing a workout, reading for ten minutes, or reaching out to someone who inspires you, let this goal represent your commitment to growth. Celebrate showing up, and trust that each choice builds momentum.

TODAY'S AFFIRMATION

I choose greatness in every small step I take.

JAN
FEB
MAR
APR
MAY
JUN
JUL
AUG
SEP
OCT
NOV
DEC

May 20

HONOR YOUR VISION

"Believe in your vision even if you're the only one who can see it."

—EVAN CARMICHAEL

Your vision deserves priority in your life. When you honor your needs and dreams first, you gain energy, clarity, and purpose, creating a ripple effect that benefits everyone around you. Today's quote reminds you to put yourself on your schedule—design a day that aligns with your vision, even if it's just for you. Putting yourself first isn't selfish; it's self-sustaining.

TODAY'S ACTION

Design a schedule that prioritizes you. Start by listing what matters most to you—activities that bring you joy, energize you or support your growth. Schedule these activities during the times when you're most focused and alert. Give yourself your best hours, then arrange other commitments around them. This slight shift is a powerful act of self-care that strengthens you to show up better for others. As you do this, you set an example for everyone in your life, showing them the value of honoring themselves.

TODAY'S AFFIRMATION

I prioritize my vision, creating a life that reflects my dreams and values.

May 21

ART FOR THE SOUL

"Art washes away from the soul the dust of everyday life."

—PABLO PICASSO

Art is a powerful source of inspiration and renewal.
Engaging with art, whether creating or simply admiring, can clear your mind, reduce stress, and bring a sense of calm and joy. Studies reveal that viewing and creating art offers cognitive and emotional benefits, helping us feel grounded and uplifted. Art invites beauty into our lives, washing away the "dust" of routine and connecting us to something more profound.

TODAY'S ACTION

Take time today to add or update a piece of art in one of your favorite rooms. It could be a photo, painting, decor item, or anything that sparks joy and reflects your style. If you feel inspired, you might buy a new piece, rearrange something from another space, or even create it yourself. This small change can transform the atmosphere of your space and add a fresh layer of beauty to your day.

TODAY'S AFFIRMATION

I surround myself with art that uplifts and inspires me.

JAN

FEB

MAR

APR

MAY

JUN

JUL

AUG

SEP

OCT

NOV

DEC

May 22

CULTIVATE COURAGE

"You gain strength, courage, and confidence by every experience in which you stop to look fear in the face."

—ELEANOR ROOSEVELT

Courage isn't about living without fear—it's about facing fear head-on. Each time you confront a challenge, no matter how small, you build resilience and confidence. Courage grows from acknowledging your fears and choosing to move forward anyway. When you cultivate bravery daily, you'll feel stronger and more positive, ready to embrace all life offers.

TODAY'S ACTION

Think of a tiny thing holding you back due to fear or hesitation. It might be starting a conversation, sharing an idea, or trying something new. Challenge yourself to take a step toward it today—expand your comfort zone. Feel the courage as you take this action head-on, knowing each step builds a stronger, more confident you.

TODAY'S AFFIRMATION

I am filled with courage in all areas of my life.

May 23

MEDIA-FREE MOMENTS

"Sometimes the best solution is to rest, relax, and recharge. It's hard to be your best on empty."

—SAM GLENN

Unplugging helps us recharge and reconnect with what truly matters. Constant scrolling and consuming information can drain our energy. Today's quote reminds us that it's hard to be our best when empty. Sometimes, the best thing we can do is step back, pause, and allow ourselves a moment to breathe. Taking a break from screens opens space to refuel, rediscover joy, and focus on the things that genuinely fulfill us.

TODAY'S ACTION

Set aside your devices for most of the day. If you need them for work, silence social media and entertainment apps and sites. Use this time to reconnect with yourself. Ask questions like: "What would feel joyful?" "How can I recharge my energy today?" Then, follow where these answers lead—whether it's spending time outside, diving into a hobby, or simply resting.

TODAY'S AFFIRMATION

I choose peace, rest, and what nurtures my well-being.

JAN

FEB

MAR

APR

MAY

JUN

JUL

AUG

SEP

OCT

NOV

DEC

May 24

DANCE WITH JOY

"When you're ready to get down and shake it up, dance like nobody's watching."

—Britney Spears

Dancing lights up your life and your spirit. You are moving to music that releases feel-good endorphins, lifting your mood and bringing pure joy. Dancing strengthens your body, sharpens your mind, and reduces stress. It's an instant energy boost, a mood enhancer, and a celebration of life. When you dance, you connect with your creativity and let positivity flow through you. Dance like nobody's watching and feel the magic it brings!

TODAY'S ACTION

Put on a song that makes you feel alive, and give yourself a few minutes to dance like nobody's watching. If you need more time to feel productive, dance and listen while tidying up or doing the dishes. If you're with family or friends, invite them to join you! Let loose, let the music take over, and notice how energized and uplifted you feel.

TODAY'S AFFIRMATION

I celebrate life, feeling alive, connected, and at peace with my body.

May 25

SHINE WITH POSITIVITY

"Don't just exist—live fully, love deeply, and let your light shine."

—KRISTEN BUTLER

Life is meant to be celebrated, not just endured. Don't let anything dim your light. Today, make it your mission to radiate love, gratitude, and positivity! Tap into your inner light and let it shine to inspire and uplift those around you. Remember, your joy creates a ripple effect that radiates to everyone around you.

TODAY'S ACTION

As a birthday gift to me (yes, today's my birthday!), celebrate yourself in a way that fills you with positivity. Choose something that makes you feel alive—dance, spend time with loved ones, laugh, or treat yourself to something special. Let positivity be your guide today, and end with gratitude by writing down three moments that made you smile.

TODAY'S AFFIRMATION

I live fully, love deeply, and shine my light brightly.

JAN

FEB

MAR

APR

MAY

JUN

JUL

AUG

SEP

OCT

NOV

DEC

May 26

WRITE YOUR STORY

"You can make anything by writing."

—C.S. Lewis

Writing opens up endless possibilities. With a pen and paper, you can explore your thoughts, capture your memories, and give voice to your dreams. Writing helps us make sense of the world. Research shows that putting thoughts to paper organizes our ideas and profoundly affects our mental clarity and emotional well-being. Writing shapes our inner thoughts, helping us process emotions, track growth, and make peace with the past.

TODAY'S ACTION

Set aside time to write freely today. Whether it's a few lines in a journal, an idea for an article, or the beginning of a book, writing can change you from the inside out. It's your story to share, explore, and bring to life. Consider reflecting on a memory, jotting down a story idea, or exploring a message you feel called to share. There's no need for perfection—just let the words flow and enjoy the process.

TODAY'S AFFIRMATION

I believe in the power of my words.

May 27

PRACTICE POSITIVITY

"Positivity is like a muscle. The more you use it, the stronger it becomes."

—JON GORDON

Positivity is a choice you make every day. When you practice positivity, you build resilience, see opportunities even in challenging situations, and create a ripple effect that impacts everyone around you. Like building strength in the gym, practicing positivity takes intention and consistency. By actively choosing a positive outlook, you're nurturing a mindset that invites more joy, hope, and gratitude into your life.

TODAY'S ACTION

Today, start the "Practice Positivity Challenge." Try three simple actions:
- Write down three things you're grateful for this morning.
- Pause midday to reflect on one positive moment.
- Share a kind word with someone today.

TODAY'S AFFIRMATION

I practice positivity, and it strengthens me daily.

JAN

FEB

MAR

APR

MAY

JUN

JUL

AUG

SEP

OCT

NOV

DEC

May 28

FOCUS BRINGS FLOW

"Focus on being productive instead of busy."

—TIM FERRISS

Flow is the zone where focus comes effortlessly, and everything seems to align. Ironically, we have to be highly focused to get in flow. That's where we can truly be productive instead of busy. In flow, creativity peaks, distractions fade, and time slips away. You can put effort into what truly matters. This state is about more than managing time. It's about managing attention and letting go of interruptions to show up with your best energy.

TODAY'S ACTION

Create a distraction-free space today. Silence notifications, clear your workspace, and set a timer for 30 minutes to focus on one priority. Permit yourself to be fully present. When the timer's up, note how much you accomplished in uninterrupted focus—prime yourself for flow every day with this simple habit.

TODAY'S AFFIRMATION

I focus my energy on what matters most.

May 29

KINDNESS IS STRENGTH

"Carry out a random act of kindness, with no expectation of reward, safe in the knowledge that one day someone might do the same for you."

—Princess Diana

Kindness is a quiet yet profound strength. How we treat others reveals our character. When we lead with compassion and understanding, we elevate our connections and create an uplifting environment for everyone around us. No matter how small, acts of kindness ripple out and inspire positivity in ways we may never fully realize.

TODAY'S ACTION

Make a conscious effort to show kindness today, whether by offering a sincere compliment, helping someone in need or simply listening without distraction. Let this act be spontaneous and heartfelt, a reminder that the smallest acts of kindness make the biggest difference.

TODAY'S AFFIRMATION

I lead with kindness, creating a positive impact wherever I go.

May 30

BELIEVE IN YOUR WORTH

"Doubt can only win if you let it. Believe in yourself, and trust that you have everything you need to succeed."

—Jamie Kern Lima

Self-belief is the foundation of all achievement. When you believe in yourself, you empower your dreams and open doors to new possibilities. Doubt may try to whisper its limitations, but by focusing on your strengths, you can overcome obstacles with resilience and courage. Remember, belief isn't about being sure of every step; it's about trusting that you'll figure things out along the way.

TODAY'S ACTION

Today, take one small step that aligns with a personal goal. Whether it's writing down an action plan, reaching out for support, or simply affirming your worth, let this step remind you of your strength and potential. Each small act of belief moves you closer to your dreams.

TODAY'S AFFIRMATION

I trust in my abilities and know I can achieve my dreams.

JAN
FEB
MAR
APR
MAY
JUN
JUL
AUG
SEP
OCT
NOV
DEC

May 31

PLAY THE LONG GAME

"A short-term gain is a long-term pain."

—Christopher A. Panagiotu

Real success isn't built on shortcuts. The most meaningful growth comes from consistent, intentional effort daily. It takes patience. Quick wins may feel good now, but they often come at the cost of real success and fulfillment. When you commit to steady, purpose-driven actions, you create a foundation for lasting growth and a life you're proud to live.

TODAY'S ACTION

Reflect on one area in your life where you can shift from short-term thinking to long-term growth. Take one small step today—whether it's saving instead of spending, investing in a relationship, or committing to personal development. These consistent actions build the foundation for sustainable success. For accountability, share your new action steps with someone you trust.

TODAY'S AFFIRMATION

I focus on long-term growth, knowing my consistent efforts create lasting success.

June

June 1

REFRAME YOUR THOUGHTS

"When you change the way you look at things,
the things you look at change."

—WAYNE DYER

The way you think shapes everything you see, feel, and experience. Your perspective can either be your prison or your passport. When you reframe your thoughts positively, you open up to new possibilities. Negative or limiting thoughts can hold you back, but with a slight shift, even the most challenging situations can reveal growth, resilience, and unexpected blessings. Every moment offers a chance to choose thoughts that uplift and empower you.

TODAY'S ACTION

Pick one recurring negative thought today and reframe it into something more supportive. Instead of thinking, "This is too hard," try, "This challenge is helping me grow." Repeat this new thought each time the opposing one surfaces, and notice how it transforms your energy and outlook.

TODAY'S AFFIRMATION

I choose thoughts that lift me and move me forward.

JAN

FEB

MAR

APR

MAY

JUN

JUL

AUG

SEP

OCT

NOV

DEC

June 2

BRAIN DUMP

"Journaling is like whispering to one's self and listening
at the same time."

—Mina Murray

A cluttered mind makes it hard to stay present. Brain
dumping is a simple, powerful way to clear mental space
by getting everything on paper. This process lets you
release thoughts, tasks, or worries weighing on your mind,
freeing you for deeper focus and flow. Writing down your
thoughts externalizes them, bringing clarity and calm. As
you see everything before you, you can quickly prioritize
and feel greater control and lightness.

TODAY'S ACTION

Set aside 10-15 minutes to do a brain dump. Sit down
with a pen and paper, minimize distractions, and write
down everything on your mind—no filters, no judgment.
Capture all the ideas, tasks, or worries that pop up.
Notice how letting it all out gives you clarity and
readiness for the day.

TODAY'S AFFIRMATION

When I clear my mind, I make space for calm and clarity.

June 3

NURTURE YOURSELF

"How you love yourself is how you teach others to love you."

—RUPI KAUR

Self-care isn't a luxury—it's a necessity. Just as you recharge your phone, taking time to unplug and nurture yourself restores your energy, focus, and resilience. When you prioritize self-care, you can be the best self for everyone around you. Making time to rest, rejuvenate, and care for your needs is essential to maintaining positivity, creativity, and balance.

TODAY'S ACTION

Treat yourself to a mini self-care break today. You could savor a quiet cup of tea, take a warm bath, walk in nature, or meditate. The key is to focus on the present moment and permit yourself to be without distractions or demands. If you need routine self-care, join the free challenge at 7daysofselfcare.com and make it a habit.

TODAY'S AFFIRMATION

I honor my needs and recharge my spirit with self-care.

JAN

FEB

MAR

APR

MAY

JUN

JUL

AUG

SEP

OCT

NOV

DEC

June 4

HONOR THE VALUE OF HARD WORK

"Anything in life worth having is worth working for."

—ANDREW CARNEGIE

A deep level of fulfillment comes from giving your best effort. Hard work is more than just picking tasks off a list. It's a way of honoring your commitments and respecting yourself. A strong work ethic is the foundation of a meaningful life. Each time you approach a task with dedication, you're not just creating results—you're building resilience, character, and a legacy of strength.

TODAY'S ACTION

Choose a task today where you can go the extra mile. Put in extra care, attention, or creativity—not to overextend yourself, but to experience the satisfaction of genuinely giving your best. Notice the feeling that comes from going above and beyond, knowing you're building resilience and leaving a mark of excellence in everything you do.

TODAY'S AFFIRMATION

I honor the value of excellence and hard work.

June 5

CHANGE YOUR THOUGHTS, CHANGE YOUR LIFE

"The greatest discovery of my generation is that a human being can alter his life by altering his attitudes."

—WILLIAM JAMES

Our thoughts shape how we experience life. Even when it doesn't feel like it, we can choose the direction of our thoughts. Cognitive Behavioral Therapy CBT) teaches us that identifying and reframing unhelpful thoughts can create a more positive mindset. This shift can ease stress, build resilience, and improve our well-being. Rather than letting worries take over, we can guide our thoughts to support our peace and positivity.

TODAY'S ACTION

Try a simple CBT technique today. Choose one recurring negative thought you've noticed. Please write it down, then re-rame it into a more positive statement. For example, if you think, "I always mess up," reframe it as, "I am learning and growing, and each mistake brings me closer to my goals." Notice how this shift in perspective lifts your mood and brings a sense of calm. Keep this nearby so you can flip the switch. Repetition is critical to change.

TODAY'S AFFIRMATION

I choose thoughts that support my growth and happiness.

June 6

SPARK A CHAIN OF KINDNESS

"Kindness is free to give, but priceless to receive."

—Raktivist

Kindness has the power to transform lives. A thoughtful gesture can brighten someone's day, inspire hope, or remind them they're not alone. And here's the magic: kindness lifts the giver as much as the receiver. When you choose to spread kindness, you're contributing to a ripple of positivity that touches everyone it reaches. It's proof that the simplest acts—a smile, a kind word, a helping hand—can create extraordinary change.

TODAY'S ACTION

Commit to one act of kindness today. Compliment someone, send a heartfelt message, or offer help where needed. Notice the joy it brings to both you and the recipient. Kindness can grow, so let your action inspire others to pass it on.

TODAY'S AFFIRMATION

I give kindness freely, knowing it creates priceless connections and spreads joy.

CONNECT WITH YOUR INNER CHILD

"Play is the highest form of research."

—ALBERT EINSTEIN

Play is a doorway to positivity. It's not just for children. Play allows creativity, curiosity, and emotional healing at any age. Reconnecting with your playful side reduces stress, boosts creativity, and strengthens problem-solving skills. Engaging your inner child is a powerful form of self-care, allowing you to release worries and rediscover a sense of wonder.

TODAY'S ACTION

Today, give yourself permission to engage in a childhood activity you loved. Whether drawing, playing a game, jumping rope, or even a playful "dance-off" in your living room, allow yourself to be present, silly, and accessible. If any memories or emotions exist, welcome them as part of the healing process. Notice how reconnecting with childlike joy brings positive energy and relaxation.

TODAY'S AFFIRMATION

I honor my playful side by embracing positivity and creativity.

JAN

FEB

MAR

APR

MAY

JUN

JUL

AUG

SEP

OCT

NOV

DEC

June 8

REFINE YOUR VISION

"Don't let short-term failures cloud your vision. Every stumble is a stepping stone to your success."

—LAURA CASSELMAN

Your vision is a work in progress. It's not fixed. You are always learning, growing, and becoming more. Every setback and stumble refines your path, clarifying what truly matters. When you view challenges as stepping stones, you better understand your goals and how to reach them. By refining your vision, you align your future with your highest intentions, transforming obstacles into opportunities for growth and gratitude.

TODAY'S ACTION

Reflect on your current vision. Consider if it still aligns with your deepest desires and long-term goals. You could even ask yourself, Is it big enough?" Take a moment to refine this vision in your journal—adjust, expand, or shift it to reflect the person you're becoming better. Embrace any setbacks you've encountered as valuable insights that guide you forward. This process sharpens your focus and permits you to dream bolder and live more intentionally.

TODAY'S AFFIRMATION

I embrace setbacks as stepping stones, refining my vision to align with my highest goals.

June 9

MOVE YOUR WAY TO POSITIVITY

"Only exercise on the days you want to be in a good mood."

—Chalene Johnson

Movement is the best mood booster. Exercise isn't just about fitness—it's about lifting your spirits, boosting your energy, and inviting joy into your day. Engaging in sports can create a sense of accomplishment and elevate your mood, building physical strength and mental resilience. Sports allow us to challenge ourselves, connect with others, and experience a pure, playful joy that stays with us long after the game.

TODAY'S ACTION

Please choose a sport that excites you and make it a part of your day! If you already have a favorite, set up a game or join a local group. If not, try something new: consider tennis, soccer, basketball, or even a fun, casual game of frisbee in the park. Challenge yourself to explore sports that energize you, with a focus on fun and community. Let this be a moment to release stress, build strength, and enjoy moving your body.

TODAY'S AFFIRMATION

I move as an essential part of my mental health and well-being.

JAN

FEB

MAR

APR

MAY

June 10

STRENGTHEN YOUR INNER RESILIENCE

"What lies behind us and what lies before us are tiny matters compared to what lies within us."

—RALPH WALDO EMERSON

True resilience comes from within. It's not about avoiding challenges but finding the strength to rise above them. When you take time to cultivate inner resilience, you tap into the deep well of strength that lies within you. Doing so helps you navigate life's ups and downs with grace. Solitude is a powerful tool for strengthening this resilience, giving you the time and space to reconnect with your inner faith and fortitude.

TODAY'S ACTION

Spend time today reflecting on a recent challenge you've faced. In a quiet, distraction-free environment, consider how you responded and what you learned about your inner strength. Write down how this experience has made you stronger, and identify any practices—such as meditation, prayer, or mindfulness—that help you maintain this resilience.

TODAY'S AFFIRMATION

I draw strength from within, knowing I have the resilience to face any challenge.

JUN

JUL

AUG

SEP

OCT

NOV

DEC

June 11

WRITE YOUR NEXT CHAPTER

"The best part about your story is that the next page is blank, and you get to write it."

—Chris Butler

Each new day is a blank page, ready to be filled with your intentions and choices. This perspective reminds us that our past doesn't dictate our future. Instead, each day allows us to shape our lives in ways that align with our dreams and values. When we see each day as a chance to write a new chapter, we empower ourselves to move forward with purpose and positivity.

TODAY'S ACTION

Take a few moments to reflect on the "next page" of your story. Set an intention for the day ahead, thinking about what you'd like to experience or accomplish. Write down one small step you can take toward your goals, visualize the outcome you're working toward, and then take one small action step today. Remember, each day is a fresh start. You hold the pen. Please don't wait for it, start today.

TODAY'S AFFIRMATION

I am the author of my life, and I write each day with purposeful action.

JAN

FEB

MAR

APR

MAY

JUN

JUL

AUG

SEP

OCT

NOV

DEC

June 12

TRY A NEW FOOD

"Cooking is a form of therapy. Get in the kitchen, connect
with your food, and nourish your body and soul."

—Dr. Uma Naidoo

**Exploring new foods is a simple way to bring adventure
into your life.** Food nourishes more than just the body;
it connects us to cultures, stories, and flavors from
around the world. Every new dish is a chance to broaden
your perspective. Expanding your culinary comfort
zone can be a fun, fulfilling way to spark creativity and
invite positivity.

TODAY'S ACTION

Try a new food today. Cook a new dish, visit a restaurant
serving a cuisine you've never tried, pick up a fruit or
vegetable you've never tasted, or experiment with a fresh
spice you've never used. Let yourself savor the experience
and enjoy the sense of discovery that comes with it.

TODAY'S AFFIRMATION

I welcome new experiences that nourish my body, mind,
and spirit.

June 13

LOVE AS YOU ARE LOVED

"We love because He first loved us."

—1 JOHN 4:19

Real love begins with God's love for you. Because He loved us first, we learn to love ourselves and reflect that love to others. Yet, expressing love to those around us is easier than to ourselves. That's because this world is full of lies telling us we are not worthy. But here's the truth: you are the one who knows yourself best—you see your strengths, your uniqueness, and everything that makes you unique. Embracing God's love lets you appreciate how He's made you beautifully and wonderfully. Writing a love letter to yourself is a powerful way to remind yourself of your worth and everything that makes you unique.

TODAY'S ACTION

When was the last time you showed yourself love? Today, write a heartfelt letter to yourself as if you were someone who loves you deeply. Express everything you admire, appreciate, and adore about who you are. Be specific, be kind, and don't hold back. This letter is a gift to you— something to cherish and reread whenever you need a boost of love.

TODAY'S AFFIRMATION

I love and accept myself, reflecting the love I receive from God.

JAN

FEB

MAR

APR

MAY

JUN

JUL

AUG

SEP

OCT

NOV

DEC

June 14

BUILD MEANINGFUL CONNECTIONS

"You have to love people; if you don't, you can't lead them."

—DONALD TRUMP

At the heart of all success is genuine connection.
Building strong personal or professional relationships comes from caring about others and uplifting them. When you take time to listen, compliment, and encourage, you create a foundation of trust and respect that strengthens every interaction. Studies show that fostering positive connections can improve mental health, boost resilience, and even enhance overall life satisfaction. Genuine connection isn't just a skill; it's an act of kindness.

TODAY'S ACTION

Today, reach out to someone you appreciate but have not connected with recently. Send a compliment, acknowledge their strengths, or check in to ask how they're doing. Notice the warmth and positivity that arises when you connect from a place of genuine care. This small gesture can strengthen your relationship and brighten both of your days.

TODAY'S AFFIRMATION

I build meaningful connections and bring kindness to every relationship.

June 15

LISTEN TO CONNECT

"Most people do not listen with the intent to understand; they listen with the intent to reply."

—Stephen R. Covey

Listening deeply is an act of connection and empathy. In a world of noise, practicing the art of listening allows us to understand others and even ourselves. When we listen thoroughly, we create space for meaningful relationships and allow ourselves to learn from others. Listening isn't just about hearing words but connecting with our hearts and minds.

TODAY'S ACTION

Practice active listening today to actively connect. When in conversation, pause to listen without forming a response. Resist the urge to interrupt and focus instead on fully absorbing the person's message. Try to understand them deeply, whether it's a friend, a family member, or a colleague. Let this remind you of the power of presence and how listening can bring you closer to those you care about.

TODAY'S AFFIRMATION

I am fully present with those around me.

JAN

FEB

MAR

APR

MAY

JUN

JUL

AUG

SEP

OCT

NOV

DEC

June 16

HEALTHY GUT, HAPPY LIFE

"To control your mind, start with your gut. It shapes your mood, cravings and behavior."

—DR. AMY SHAH

Your gut is the gateway to your mind and mood. A balanced gut microbiome fuels mental clarity, boosts mood, and strengthens immunity. When your gut thrives, your whole body benefits—supporting digestion, nutrient absorption, and emotional well-being. Prioritize your gut health for a healthier, happier you.

TODAY'S ACTION

Boost your gut health by incorporating a variety of nutrient-dense foods, adding probiotics and prebiotics, and reducing processed foods and sugar. Start today by making one or two of these changes, and aim to keep adding more daily. Notice how these simple choices impact your digestion, mood, and energy over time. Prioritizing your gut health can lead to lasting improvements in your overall well-being.

TODAY'S AFFIRMATION

I eat foods that support my health, inside and out.

June 17

STAY TRUE TO YOUR PATH

"Always stay true to yourself and never let what
somebody says distract you from your goals."

—MICHELLE OBAMA

Your path is uniquely yours. In a world of opinions,
getting sidetracked or doubting yourself is easy. But true
success comes when y u stay aligned with your values
and goals, regardless of others' opinions. When you honor
your path and remain focused, you create a genuinely
fulfilling and authentic life—staying true to yourself isn't
just about ignoring distractions but embracing the
courage to follow your heart.

TODAY'S ACTION

Take a few moments to reconnect with your goals and
values. Write down one or two key goals that matter
most to you and reflect on why they're essential. Let this
remind you what you're working toward and why it's
meaningful. If any outside opinions or distractions have
been weighing on you, choose to release them. Return to
your path with a renewed sense of focus and clarity.

TODAY'S AFFIRMATION

I stay true to myself and focus on my goals, creating a life
that aligns with my purpose.

June 18

CREATE YOUR FUTURE

"Your dream job doesn't exist. You have to create it."

—JESS EKSTROM

The life of your dreams is waiting to be built. Fulfillment comes when you stop searching and start crafting your desired reality, one choice at a time. Each step expands your comfort zone and brings you closer to what once seemed impossible. When you create what doesn't yet exist, you become the architect of a life that feels authentically, powerfully yours.

TODAY'S ACTION

Try a "Future Letter" exercise to connect with your vision. In a quiet spot, imagine yourself in the future, living your dream life. Write a letter as this future version of you—describe what you've achieved, your life, and the wisdom you'd share. Let yourself feel the pride of reaching these goals as if they're happening now. This step fuels your motivation and clarifies your dreams.

TODAY'S AFFIRMATION

I am the creator of my reality.

JAN
FEB
MAR
APR
MAY
JUN
JUL
AUG
SEP
OCT
NOV
DEC

June 19

LAUGH OUT LOUD

"Life is worth living as long as there's a laugh in it."

—L.M. Montgomery

Silliness is a powerful mood booster and a path to creativity. Being playful disrupts our usual thinking, freeing us to see things from a fresh perspective. Embracing silliness brings laughter and lightness and helps us connect deeply with others. Plus, playfulness sparks creativity, leading to out-of-the-box ideas, solutions, and opportunities.

TODAY'S ACTION

Today, give yourself permission to be as silly. Laugh out loud, dance around, tell a funny joke, talk in an accent, or make a goofy song. Let your playful side shine. If you're with friends or family, invite them to join in. Let go of inhibitions and notice how your mood lifts as you embody this playful energy. Laughter and joy are some of life's best medicines, so let yourself be fully in the moment.

TODAY'S AFFIRMATION

I allow my playfulness to bring me joy.

JAN

FEB

MAR

APR

MAY

JUN

JUL

AUG

SEP

OCT

NOV

DEC

June 20

PAUSE TO SEE THE GOOD

"Taking a true break helps you to come back with a clear mind and clear direction on what needs to get done!"

—Elisha Covey

Sometimes, the best way to find positivity is to step back. In our busy lives, getting overwhelmed by the constant stream of tasks, notifications, and news is easy. But when you pause and take a genuine break, you create space to see the good hidden in plain sight. A proper break can help clear your mind, lift your mood, and refocus your energy on what truly matters.

TODAY'S ACTION

Permit yourself to take a real break today. Step away from your routine,   put down your phone, and breathe. Use this time to notice something positive—a small act of kindness, peace, or something that brings you joy. Let this break help you reset, recharge, and refocus on the good.

TODAY'S AFFIRMATION

I find clarity and joy when I take a moment to pause.

June 21

RECHARGE WITH SOLITUDE

"I never found a companion that was so companionable as solitude."

—HENRY DAVID THOREAU

Solitude is a powerful way to reconnect with yourself.
In the hustle of life, it's easy to forget your own needs,
always prioritizing everyone else over yourself. But
remember, taking time for yourself is a necessity. It's
about honoring your inner world, listening to your voice,
and reconnecting with what makes you feel alive. A few
moments of solitude can help you recharge, find clarity,
and rediscover your inner peace.

TODAY'S ACTION

When was the last time you took time for yourself? Today,
carve out some alone time just for you. Choose activities
that nourish your soul for 30 minutes, a few hours, or
a whole day. Read a book, pray, meditate, walk, or sit
silently. Make this time free of distractions and external
pressures, and allow yourself to breathe, reflect, and
reconnect. You deserve this time, and your well-being will
be a source of gratitude.

TODAY'S AFFIRMATION

I honor my needs and create space for peace in my life.

JAN

FEB

MAR

APR

MAY

JUN

JUL

AUG

SEP

OCT

NOV

DEC

June 22

EXPRESS YOUR APPRECIATION

"Love and gratitude are the words that must serve as the guide for the world."

—Dr. Masaru Emoto

Showing appreciation lifts both the giver and receiver. When you take a moment to recognize the qualities you admire in someone else, you also affirm those qualities within yourself. This is why it feels so fulfilling to appreciate the people who bring value and joy into your life.

TODAY'S ACTION

Think of someone you genuinely admire and appreciate. Make a list of all the qualities you love about them—either as a list or a heartfelt letter. Notice how uplifting it feels to shower them with appreciation and gratitude. If you can, consider reaching out to share your words with them. Experience the warmth and connection that come from expressing your gratitude openly.

TODAY'S AFFIRMATION

I nurture my relationships with love, gratitude, and appreciation.

June 23

POWER IN PURPOSE

"Your purpose is your source of power."

—EVAN CARMICHAEL

Purpose is the fuel that drives you forward. Connecting with what truly matters unlocks strength, resilience, and positivity. Purpose brings meaning to each day, inspiring actions that align with your highest self. Living with purpose not only empowers you but uplifts those around you.

TODAY'S ACTION

Start a "Purpose Power Hour" by setting aside one hour today to focus intensely on a goal or passion that resonates with you. Begin by writing down a specific step—such as researching a topic, outlining a project, or reaching out to someone who inspires you. During this hour, commit fully, free from distractions, and feel the momentum from aligning with your purpose. Schedule a daily "PPH" to stay connected to your purpose through focused action if it resonates.

TODAY'S AFFIRMATION

My purpose fills me with strength and clarity.

LIVE YOUR FAITH

"Faith without works is dead."

—James 2:26

Faith alone is a spark, but action brings it to life. It's not enough to believe. We must show our faith through what we do. When you put faith into action, you align your life with what you trust most. Each step in faith becomes a statement of your beliefs—a light that guides you and inspires others. True faith is active, intentional, and transformative.

TODAY'S ACTION

Identify one area where you can put your faith into action. Whether helping someone, starting a new project, prioritizing health, or making a tough decision, take a step today that reflects your trust in God's plan. Let your actions be a living testament to your faith.

TODAY'S AFFIRMATION

I let my faith guide my actions, bringing purpose and light into my life.

JAN
FEB
MAR
APR
MAY
JUN
JUL
AUG
SEP
OCT
NOV
DEC

June 25

WALK WITH PURPOSE

"Walking is man's best medicine."

—Hippocrates

Each step forward is a step toward vitality. Power walking is more than just movement; it's an active, purposeful way to boost your health, mood, and energy. Walking with intention fuels your heart, strengthens your muscles, and uplifts your spirit. Brisk walking offers a simple yet powerful way to improve your stamina and focus, leaving you feeling positive and refreshed.

TODAY'S ACTION

Try a 15-20 minute power walk. If that's too easy, challenge yourself for 45-60 minutes. Begin with a warm-up at a leisurely pace, then gradually pick up speed to reach a brisk, strong stride. Engage your core, keep your spine straight, and let your arms swing naturally. Focus on your breathing, making each inhale and exhale rhythmic and deep. As you finish, slow down to a relaxed stroll and take a few moments to stretch. Feel how this energizes you, and let each step remind you of your strength and vitality.

TODAY'S AFFIRMATION

I walk with strength and purpose toward my best self.

JAN

FEB

MAR

APR

MAY

JUN

JUL

AUG

SEP

OCT

NOV

DEC

June 26

FOCUS FOR SUCCESS

"Success demands singleness of purpose."

—Vince Lombardi

True success starts with unwavering focus. When you commit fully to a single purpose, distractions fade, and your energy flows toward what matters most. This focused intention turns dreams into achievable goals and empowers you to accomplish things you never thought possible. By centering your attention on what truly matters, you create momentum, clarity, and the power to make meaningful progress.

TODAY'S ACTION

Choose one goal or task today that aligns with your bigger purpose. Block out distractions and silence notifications, and give this goal your full attention for a set time. Notice how staying focused on this single purpose makes you feel more capable and connected to your path.

TODAY'S AFFIRMATION

I focus my energy on what truly matters and move confidently toward my goals.

LABEL YOUR EMOTIONS

"To label your feelings is to take away their power over you. It's the first step towards emotional freedom."

—Rose Scott

Labeling your emotions brings clarity and calm.
Research shows that identifying and naming your emotions can reduce their intensity and help you manage them more effectively. By simply labeling what you feel, you activate areas of the brain associated with emotional regulation, creating space to respond thoughtfully instead of impulsively. This practice builds emotional resilience, enabling you to handle challenges more easily.

TODAY'S ACTION

Create an "Emotions List" on your phone's notes and keep track throughout the day. Each time you feel a strong emotion, pause and label it—happy, frustrated, excited, anxious. Jot down the word briefly on your list, and notice how putting a name to it helps you handle it more easily. Repeat this practice with different emotions to build emotional awareness and control.

TODAY'S AFFIRMATION

I gain strength and clarity by recognizing and naming my emotions.

JAN

FEB

MAR

APR

MAY

JUN

JUL

AUG

SEP

OCT

NOV

DEC

June 28

CHOOSE TO BE EXTRAORDINARY

"It is possible for ordinary people to choose to be extraordinary."

—ELON MUSK

Every extraordinary journey starts with a simple choice. It's not talent or luck that makes the difference—it's the decision to push beyond the ordinary. When you choose to be extraordinary, you commit to growth, resilience, and taking bold steps toward your potential. Success isn't about following a formula; it's about believing in yourself and showing up daily. You don't need a perfect plan—just a willingness to grow and make each day count.

TODAY'S ACTION

Expand your comfort zone with an "Extraordinary Action." Choose one goal you've been hesitant about, and take a bold step toward it. Pick something that feels ambitious yet exciting. Let this action ignite your journey toward greatness, whether reaching out to a mentor, learning a new skill, starting a project, or setting a personal best.

TODAY'S AFFIRMATION

I choose to be extraordinary and take bold steps towards my highest potential.

June 29

CREATE YOUR BRIGHTER FUTURE

"Instead of looking at what's depressing, look at what's a blessing."

—Kristen Butler

Your thoughts today are seeds for tomorrow's reality. When you focus on what's going right, you build the foundation for a future filled with positivity and purpose. Science shows a positive outlook can boost health, resilience, and success. By choosing to see your blessings instead of your burdens, you're inviting more opportunities into your life. The more you celebrate the good, the more it grows.

TODAY'S ACTION

Start a "Blessings List" today. Each time you experience something positive, no matter how small—write it down in a notebook or your phone. At day's end, read through your list and let it lift you. This practice will train your mind to notice the good and reinforce the positivity in your life, helping you create a brighter future.

TODAY'S AFFIRMATION

I focus on my blessings to create a brighter, more positive future.

JAN

FEB

MAR

APR

MAY

JUN

JUL

AUG

SEP

OCT

NOV

DEC

June 30

CONSISTENCY IS KEY

"What you do every day matters more than
what you do once in a while."

—Gretchen Rubin

**True success is built on the steady, daily steps that
shape our future.** Every small, consistent action adds
up over time, creating a life of purpose and positivity. By
choosing long-term growth over instant gratification, we
set ourselves toward a more fulfilling future. Consistency
isn't about perfection; it's the commitment to show
up each day and make choices that align with who
you're becoming.

TODAY'S ACTION

Identify one area where you want to grow. Choose one
small, meaningful action that aligns with this goal—
reading a few pages, setting aside time for reflection,
or enjoying a walk outdoors. Commit to doing this daily,
no matter how small it may feel, and observe how each
day's progress brings you closer to your vision. Over time,
consistency will make each step lighter and each goal
more attainable.

TODAY'S AFFIRMATION

I choose long-term growth over instant gratification by
taking steady, consistent action.

July

July 1

EMBRACE YOUR FREEDOM

"Freedom lies in being bold."

—Robert Frost

True freedom comes from within. It's the courage to live authentically, make choices aligned with your values, and pursue what brings you joy and meaning. Freedom isn't just about physical boundaries—it's about releasing limiting beliefs, self-doubt, and anything that holds you back. When you embrace this inner freedom, you open the door to a life filled with purpose and possibility.

TODAY'S ACTION

Reflect on one area in your life where you can cultivate more freedom. This could be setting a boundary, letting go of an old belief, or stepping toward a goal you've been holding back on. Write down one bold action you can take today to embrace your freedom—no matter how small—and commit to it. Every step you take toward your authentic self expands your freedom.

TODAY'S AFFIRMATION

I am free to live boldly, embracing each day with courage and authenticity.

INSTANT POSITIVITY **203**

JAN
FEB
MAR
APR
MAY
JUN
JUL
AUG
SEP
OCT
NOV
DEC

FOCUS ON SELF-ACCEPTANCE

"It's not your job to like me —it's mine."

—Byron Katie

Freedom is found in self-acceptance, not others' approval. How much energy do you spend trying to be liked? Many seek approval, adjust to fit in, or gain acceptance. Letting go of the need for external validation creates space to celebrate who you are—quirks, strengths, and all. Embracing self-acceptance builds an inner strength that brightens your life and brings lasting positivity.

TODAY'S ACTION

Create a "Confidence Boost List." Write down three things you genuinely like about yourself—qualities, talents, or traits. Be specific. Keep this list nearby, and whenever you feel the urge to seek approval, read it aloud as a reminder of your worth. Make this a daily habit, and watch your confidence grow.

TODAY'S AFFIRMATION

I celebrate who I am, confident in my worth and value.

July 3

BUILD CORE CONFIDENCE

"Your core is your body's powerhouse. Strengthen it, and every move you make becomes easier and more effective."

—TONY HORTON

A strong core is the foundation of a strong life. It houses vital organs, connects your limbs, and supports your posture. Strengthening your core sets you up for a healthier, more active life—allowing you to do more, feel energized, and enjoy each moment. Studies show that a strong core is linked to better health and longevity. Your core protects against injury and supports a positive, active life as you age.

TODAY'S ACTION

Build core strength today with a plank. This simple, effective exercise requires no equipment, just a few minutes of focus. Find enough space to lie down, and aim for a one- or two-minute plank. Beginners can set a 30-second timer or modify it by dropping to their knees. This daily practice can boost core strength, reduce back pain risk, and improve endurance.

TODAY'S AFFIRMATION

I am getting healthier and stronger with every movement.

July 4

FREEDOM AND JOY

"The spirit of joy and the spirit of freedom go hand in hand."

—CATHERINE DOHERTY

True freedom brings a deep sense of joy. When you live freely—aligned with your values, free from fear, and open to possibility—you invite joy into your life. Freedom isn't just the absence of restrictions; true freedom begins when we let go. Many of us carry burdens that weigh us down without even realizing it—holding onto stress, worries, and past experiences. Freedom is found in the release. When we let go, we allow joy to enter. Joy and freedom thrive together.

TODAY'S ACTION

Reflect on one area in your life where you can create more freedom. Is there a limiting belief, a habit, or a worry you can release to live more joyfully? Write down one small step you can take today to bring more freedom and joy into your life—whether it's spending time doing something you love, releasing a worry, or setting a boundary that honors your well-being.

TODAY'S AFFIRMATION

I allow the spirit of freedom and joy into my life.

July 5

GIVE BACK TO GROW

"We make a living by what we get, but we make a life by what we give."

—WINSTON CHURCHILL

Volunteering is a gift that gives back in countless ways. Every act of service creates a ripple of kindness that extends far beyond the moment. When you volunteer, you're not just helping others—you're also uplifting your own life. A special kind of joy comes from knowing you've made a difference. You also discover deeper connections, new perspectives, and a sense of purpose that brings true fulfillment to your life.

TODAY'S ACTION

Take a step to give back today. If you're new to volunteering, find an organization that aligns with your passions and offer your time. If you already volunteer, consider stepping into a leadership role or exploring new ways to support your community. If you cannot donate your time, consider donating supplies or making a financial contribution. Remember, every act of service— big or small—creates a ripple of positivity that reaches far beyond what you can see.

TODAY'S AFFIRMATION

I uplift my community and enrich the world through my actions.

July 6

STRENGTHEN YOUR CORE

"The core is the center of everything. If you have a
strong core, everything else falls into place."

—SERENA WILLIAMS

**Your core isn't just physical—it's the foundation of your
well-being.** A strong physical and mental core gives you
the stability to face life's challenges with resilience and
balance. When you build strength from the inside out,
you find a sense of alignment that impacts every area of
your life, from health to relationships to personal goals.
Strengthening your core means fortifying yourself so you
can stand tall and feel grounded no matter what comes
your way.

TODAY'S ACTION

Choose one small action to strengthen your core—
physically, mentally, or emotionally. It could be a few
minutes of core exercises, a grounding meditation,
or setting a clear boundary that reinforces your inner
stability. Notice how this small action connects you to
your sense of strength and balance.

TODAY'S AFFIRMATION

I strengthen my core and build a stable foundation for
every area of my life.

IGNITE YOUR COURAGE

"Do something that scares you every day."

—ELEANOR ROOSEVELT

Adventure is a doorway to growth and self-discovery.
A spark waiting to be ignited. When we settle into
routines, that spark can start to fade, but stepping
into new experiences keeps us alive and growing. You
expand your comfort zone and strengthen your resilience
whenever you try something unfamiliar. New challenges
boost creativity and help you stay more engaged in life.

TODAY'S ACTION

Pick one activity that excites or challenges you—a new
class, hobby, or skill you've wanted to try. Take a small
step toward it today, or schedule it so you can look
forward to the experience. Growth starts with action, one
step at a time.

TODAY'S AFFIRMATION

I welcome new experiences that ignite my courage and
light up my life.

JAN

FEB

MAR

APR

MAY

JUN

JUL

AUG

SEP

OCT

NOV

DEC

July 8

RISE STRONG, STAND TALL

"Don't let anyone break you. There may always be people who secretly want to see you fail. That's okay. Just stay strong and stand tall."

—KRISTEN BUTLER

Standing tall isn't just about posture—it's a statement of resilience. Choosing to stand tall affirms your inner strength, even when facing challenges or doubt from others. Good posture grounds you physically and sends a powerful message: you are strong, confident, and capable. Holding your head high aligns with self-assurance, reminding yourself of your worth and ability to overcome anything.

TODAY'S ACTION

Today, embody strength through your posture. Whenever you catch yourself slouching, stand tall with shoulders back, chest open, and chin lifted. Use each adjustment as a reminder of your resilience and power. If helpful, set a timer to check in every hour. Notice how standing tall lifts your mood, sharpens your focus, and brings a sense of positivity.

TODAY'S AFFIRMATION

I stand tall and embody strength and positivity.

July 9

WRITE FOR SELF-DISCOVERY

"A journal is your completely unaltered voice."

—Lucy Dacus

Journaling is an excellent tool for self-discovery. It creates clarity around your dreams and goals. When you write down what you truly want, you claim it, giving shape and energy to your vision. Putting pen to paper connects you directly to your desires and brings you closer to the future you want to create. The clearer and more joyful you feel about your vision, the faster it can unfold.

TODAY'S ACTION

Find a quiet place with your journal, and take a few deep breaths. Then, ask yourself, "What do I truly want?" Write down your deepest desires, letting your words flow without judgment. Be honest, transparent, and as specific as feels good. As you write, tap into the feelings of fulfilling these desires—joy, excitement, freedom. If you struggle with journaling, try the 3 Minute Positivity Journal, which contains prompts and themes that are an excellent tool for self-discovery and accountability toward your growth.

TODAY'S AFFIRMATION

I write my future into being with clarity, confidence, and positivity.

JAN
FEB
MAR
APR
MAY
JUN
JUL
AUG
SEP
OCT
NOV
DEC

July 10

TAKE A BABY STEP

"You are the only person on earth who can use your ability."

—ZIG ZIGLAR

Big dreams can feel overwhelming, but every success starts with a single step. Remember, even the most significant accomplishments are achieved one small action at a time. You don't need to do it all at once—focus on the next step. With each baby step you take, you're moving closer to your dreams, and consistency will make them a reality.

TODAY'S ACTION

Break down your vision into the smallest possible action steps—tasks you can complete in a few minutes or an hour. Choose one step and accomplish it today. Celebrate this win, no matter how small. If you're feeling inspired, tackle another step and celebrate that too. Every small step adds up to significant progress.

TODAY'S AFFIRMATION

I celebrate every baby step I take toward my dreams.

July 11

CREATE EASE THROUGH ORDER

"Organization isn't about perfection; it's about reducing stress and improving life."

—CHRISTINA SCALISE

Organization is about creating ease, not perfection. An organized space is a foundation for living your best life. Studies show that reducing clutter decreases stress, boosts focus, and enhances mental clarity. When we clear out what we don't need, we invite more ease, efficiency, and positivity into our lives. Organized surroundings set the stage for a day filled with calm and purpose, helping us show up fully and creating room for growth.

TODAY'S ACTION

Take 15 minutes to declutter and refresh your car. Remove anything unnecessary, organize your needs, and tidy up the interior. Treat it to a quick car wash. Then, go for a short drive to enjoy a clean car's clarity and confidence. This simple act can set a positive, productive tone for your day!

TODAY'S AFFIRMATION

I bring calm and clarity to my life by creating order in my spaces.

JAN

FEB

MAR

APR

MAY

JUN

JUL

AUG

SEP

OCT

NOV

DEC

July 12

CREATE A VISION BOARD

"The only limit to your impact is your
imagination and commitment."

—TONY ROBBINS

**A vision board is a powerful tool for bringing your
dreams to life.** It's a visual representation of the future
you're creating, a reminder of what's possible when
you believe in your vision. Yesterday, you took time to
envision your ideal future; today, let's turn that vision into
something you can see every day, using images and
words that inspire and motivate you.

TODAY'S ACTION

Create your vision board using whatever medium feels
best—digitally on your phone or computer or traditionally
with magazine cutouts on a poster board. Place images,
words, and phrases that resonate with your goals in high-
traffic areas, like around your mirror or on your fridge.
If you're unsure where to start, consider joining the free
Vision Board Challenge at visionboardchallenge.com to
get inspired and take the first step toward your dreams.

TODAY'S AFFIRMATION

I see my dreams with clarity and commit to them
regularly.

July 13

SPREAD JOY THROUGH GIVING

"Real generosity toward the future lies in giving all to the present."

—ALBERT CAMUS

Generosity is a way of planting seeds of joy in the lives of others. Giving can uplift and create lasting positivity, whether it's your time, a small gift, or a kind gesture. Faithful giving comes without expectation to bring happiness to someone else's day. Each act of kindness builds a stronger, more connected world and reminds us that small gestures can have a significant impact.

TODAY'S ACTION

Today, find a way to give to someone in your life. It could be treating a friend to coffee, surprising a family member with a heartfelt note, or simply helping a stranger. Focus on giving purely from a place of love and kindness, without expecting anything in return. As you see the joy your generosity creates, notice how it also lifts your heart.

TODAY'S AFFIRMATION

I give freely, creating joy and positivity in the world around me.

JAN

FEB

MAR

APR

MAY

JUN

JUL

AUG

SEP

OCT

NOV

DEC

July 14

FLOW LIKE WATER

"Dance with the waves, move with the sea, let the rhythm of the water set your soul free."

—CHRISTY ANN MARTINE

Water has a natural rhythm that invites us to find our flow. Just as waves rise and fall, life has its own pace, and spending time near water can remind us to move with life's rhythm. Watching the gentle ripple of a lake, the steady river flow or the ocean's crashing waves can ease our minds and bring us into harmony with the moment. When we go with the flow, we let go of resistance and allow peace to wash over us.

TODAY'S ACTION

Find a body of water—a beach, riverbank, pond, or fountain—and let its rhythm guide you. Observe the movement, listen to the sounds, and feel the calming energy around you. Imagine yourself in sync with this flow, releasing stress with each breath. Allow the water's rhythm to help you reset and realign with the natural flow of your life.

TODAY'S AFFIRMATION

I flow with life's rhythm, finding peace and balance every moment.

FIND PEACE IN NATURE

"Nature has a way of reminding you that
everything is going to be okay."

—Robert F. Kennedy Jr.

Nature is a gentle reminder of life's steady rhythm.
In times of stress or uncertainty, stepping outside can
offer a powerful sense of calm and reassurance. The
beauty and resilience of nature—trees standing tall, rivers
flowing, birds singing—are reminders that life continues,
that challenges pass, and that peace is always within
reach.

TODAY'S ACTION

Take a few moments today to connect with nature. Step
outside, breathe deeply and let the sounds, sights, and
scents around you bring calm. Whether it's a short walk,
a moment in your garden, or even a look out the window,
allow nature to remind you that everything will be okay in
the grand scheme.

TODAY'S AFFIRMATION

I find peace and reassurance in nature's steady rhythm.

INSTANT POSITIVITY **217**

JAN
FEB
MAR
APR
MAY
JUN
JUL
AUG
SEP
OCT
NOV
DEC

July 16

BUILD STRENGTH WITH WEIGHTS

"The difference between try and triumph is a little 'umph.'"

—MARVIN PHILLIPS

Triumph comes from that extra effort that turns intention into success. It's about pushing beyond mediocrity to build grit and resilience. True strength adds positive energy to your life—lifting you above the ordinary. Weight training is a powerful way to create inner and outer strength, building your mindset, confidence, and body from the inside out. Each rep and lift brings that extra 'umph' to your day, leaving you feeling stronger, clearer, and more positive.

TODAY'S ACTION

No matter your fitness level, commit to building strength today! If you can, head to the gym and challenge yourself with weights, or use hand weights at home. Try bicep curls, shoulder presses, or lunges to target different muscle groups. Feel the power in each movement as you lift, breathe, and grow stronger. Each step you take today builds resilience and strength, bringing you closer to triumph.

TODAY'S AFFIRMATION

I am strong, resilient, and empowered inside and out.

July 17

DARE TO THINK DIFFERENTLY

"I promise you will find success when you dare to think differently."

—KENDRA SCOTT

Success comes from breaking away from conventional thinking. When you dare to approach challenges from a fresh angle, you open doors to creativity and growth. Thinking differently means trusting your unique perspective and believing new solutions are possible. This mindset helps you see opportunities where others may see limitations and allows you to build a life and career that's truly your own.

TODAY'S ACTION

Identify one area in your life where you feel stuck or limited. Challenge yourself to approach it from a new perspective. Ask, "What would this look like if I thought differently?" Write down one unique solution or idea and commit to exploring it further. Sometimes, a slight shift in thinking can lead to a significant breakthrough.

TODAY'S AFFIRMATION

Thinking differently leads me to success.

JAN

FEB

MAR

APR

MAY

JUN

JUL

AUG

SEP

OCT

NOV

DEC

July 18

LEAD BY EXAMPLE

"People are influenced more by what you DO than what you SAY. Words matter, but your example matters more."

—DANIEL DECKER

Your actions speak louder than words ever could. While words have power, your actions leave a lasting impact. By showing up authentically, staying true to your values, and living with integrity, you inspire others to do the same. Leading by example isn't just about achieving personal goals—it's about being the kind of person who uplifts and motivates those around them.

TODAY'S ACTION

Identify one area in your life where you'd like to set a positive example. This could be through kindness, resilience, or action on a goal you've been putting off. Today, show up fully in this area and let your actions reflect who you want to be. Notice how it feels to lead by example, inspiring others through your actions.

TODAY'S AFFIRMATION

I lead by example, inspiring others through my actions and integrity.

July 19

LEAD WITH CONFIDENCE

"I've learned that people want to work with others who have confidence. If you don't believe in yourself, how can anyone else?"

—Anna Costa

Confidence is magnetic. When you genuinely believe in yourself, it shows in your actions, words, and energy, inviting others to believe in you, too. Confidence isn't about perfection—it's about trusting your unique strengths and showing up with courage. The more you lean into your potential, the more others will see and support it.

TODAY'S ACTION

Create a "Confidence Card." On a small card or sticky note, jot down one strength or accomplishment that makes you proud. Keep it close—tuck it in your pocket or wallet. Before starting a task or conversation, glance at your card to reconnect with what makes you uniquely capable. Let this reminder boost your confidence and brighten each moment.

TODAY'S AFFIRMATION

I trust my strengths and lead with confidence.

JAN

FEB

MAR

APR

MAY

JUN

JUL

AUG

SEP

OCT

NOV

DEC

July 20

FOCUS ON POSITIVE OUTCOMES

"If you don't like something, change it. If you can't change it, change your attitude."

—Maya Angelou

What you focus on expands. Like attracts like. When you focus on something, you naturally see and attract more of it. This isn't just a coincidence; it's a powerful reminder that your attention shapes your reality. Focusing on positive outcomes sets the stage for more good things to flow into your life. Your actions align with your intentions.

TODAY'S ACTION

Set a "Positivity Spotlight" timer for three times today— morning, afternoon, and evening. Pause and note something positive around or within yourself each time it goes off. Jot these down, and review your list at the end of the day. Watch how focusing on the good invites more positivity into your life.

TODAY'S AFFIRMATION

I expect the best and attract positive outcomes into my life.

July 21

BUILD A POSITIVE MINDSET

"I believe if you keep your faith, you keep your trust, you keep the right attitude, if you're grateful, you'll see God open up new doors."

—JOEL OSTEEN

Affirmations are powerful tools for shaping your mindset and life. You can replace self-doubt and negative beliefs with empowering thoughts that fuel your growth by choosing intentional, positive statements. Regular affirmations can rewire your mind, helping you adopt new beliefs and attract positive outcomes.

TODAY'S ACTION

Identify one limiting belief holding you back and create a positive affirmation to counter it. For example, if you struggle with self-doubt, affirm, "I am confident and capable" or "I trust my decisions." Keep it specific, in the present tense, and repeat it throughout the day—morning, evening, or anytime you need a mindset boost.

TODAY'S AFFIRMATION

My positive mindset opens doors to new opportunities.

JAN
FEB
MAR
APR
MAY
JUN
JUL
AUG
SEP
OCT
NOV
DEC

July 22

BE A FORCE FOR GOOD

"Do your little bit of good where you are; it's those little
bits of good put together that overwhelm the world."

—DESMOND TUTU

Small actions can create powerful waves of change.
When you act with kindness and integrity, you're helping
others and adding positivity to the world. Each choice
to uplift, encourage, or support sends ripples of hope
far beyond what you may see. You inspire others to do
the same by being a force for good, creating a cycle of
positivity and compassion.

TODAY'S ACTION

Choose one action today that contributes to the
good of others—whether it's offering encouragement,
volunteering your time, or standing up for someone in
need. Take a moment to reflect on how this simple act
can create a ripple effect. If it resonates, create a list of
actions you can take regularly to send out these ripples
of hope.

TODAY'S AFFIRMATION

I am a source of hope and positivity.

July 23

QUESTION YOUR BELIEFS

"The only limit to our realization of tomorrow
will be our doubts of today."

—FRANKLIN D. ROOSEVELT

Beliefs are powerful, but they aren't facts. A belief is a thought you've repeated until it feels authentic, shaped by your own experiences—not by universal truths. Recognizing this frees you to question what you've accepted as reality, opening space for new, empowering possibilities.

TODAY'S ACTION

Choose one belief you frequently hold about yourself—something that might hold you back. Write it down and ask yourself, "Is this a fact?" If it's not true 100% of the time or can't be verified, take a moment to reframe it. Replace it with a new belief that empowers you, such as "I am capable of growth" or "I am worthy of success." Reflect on how this shift in perspective feels and carry this new belief throughout the day.

TODAY'S AFFIRMATION

I release beliefs that no longer serve me and choose empowering possibilities.

JAN

FEB

MAR

APR

MAY

JUN

JUL

AUG

SEP

OCT

NOV

DEC

July 24

THE POWER OF PERSEVERANCE

"Many of life's failures are people who did not realize
how close they were to success when they gave up."

—THOMAS EDISON

**Success is often just one step past where you feel like
giving up.** Perseverance is what expands you to that next
level. It's the fuel that takes you closer to your dreams,
especially when the journey feels challenging. You build
resilience and close in on your goals whenever you
choose to keep going. Trust that it's worth every ounce of
effort if it matters to you. Keep going—you're closer than
you think.

TODAY'S ACTION

Give yourself a 30-minute perseverance challenge.
Choose one task or goal you've been putting off. For
30 minutes, commit fully. Block out distractions, silence
doubts, and focus. When discouragement creeps in, take
a deep breath and remind yourself how far you've come.
At the end, celebrate your effort and write down one
reason why continuing is worth it.

TODAY'S AFFIRMATION

I keep moving forward, knowing success is within reach.

DIRECT YOUR DAY WITH PURPOSE

"God put you here on purpose and for a purpose."

—Jason Wolbers

Your life has a purpose. You are not here by accident. You were created with a divine purpose, a unique mission only you can fulfill. Embracing your purpose means stepping into the life you were meant to live, fully aligned with the values and passions that light up your soul. When you connect with this higher calling, you unlock a deep sense of fulfillment, joy, and direction that guides you through every challenge and opportunity. Today is a reminder that your life has meaning, and you are here to make a difference.

TODAY'S ACTION

Find a quiet space and reflect on your divine purpose. Ask yourself: What unique gifts has God given me? How can I use them to serve a higher purpose? Write down your insights. Then, choose one specific action today that aligns with your purpose: helping someone, starting a meaningful project, or committing to a daily habit that nourishes your soul.

TODAY'S AFFIRMATION

I live each day with purpose, aligning my actions with my values.

JAN

FEB

MAR

APR

MAY

JUN

JUL

AUG

SEP

OCT

NOV

DEC

July 26

PRIORITIZE FEELING BETTER

"You can't control everything that happens to you,
but you can control how you react to it."

—Lewis Howes

Your emotions are yours to shape—choose actions that uplift you. While we can't prevent every negative situation, we have power over how we respond. Emotions will rise throughout the day, but you can let them go and choose actions that boost your mood. Prioritizing your emotional health builds a strong foundation for growth. Positive emotions bring mental clarity and energy and improve relationships—with yourself and others.

TODAY'S ACTION

Make a list of activities that uplift you when you're in an emotional rut. It could be walking, spending time with loved ones, watching something funny, or listening to music. Next time you feel down, choose one activity from your list and take action toward feeling better. Each small choice toward positivity brings greatness into your life.

TODAY'S AFFIRMATION

I prioritize feeling good, knowing it strengthens every part of my life.

July 27

EMBRACE COURAGEOUS ACTION

"Courage is being scared to death but saddling up anyway."

—John Wayne

Courage is taking action, even when fear tries to hold you back. Bravery shows up quietly—in the willingness to try something new, take a step that feels risky, or stand firm in your beliefs. Each time you take a courageous action, you affirm your strength and build resilience. Actual growth happens when you take bold steps, one at a time, even if they feel small or you feel a little nervous.

TODAY'S ACTION

Choose a specific goal or situation that feels daunting. Then, break it down into smaller, bold actions. As a first step, set a timer for 10 minutes and work on one action related to that goal—sending an email, making a call, or gathering resources. Allow the timer to keep you focused, pushing aside self-doubt or hesitation. After completing it, reward yourself with something, like a favorite treat or a short break, to reinforce the positive impact of courageous action.

TODAY'S AFFIRMATION

I lead with courage, taking bold steps toward my goals with confidence.

July 28

RELEASE NEGATIVITY

"You cannot have a positive life and a negative mind."

—Joyce Meyer

Emotional baggage is heavy. You can be in the most beautiful place, surrounded by love, but if negative emotions weigh you down, they alter your perspective. Our inner world reflects our outer experience. That's why two people can go through the same event; one sees joy while the other sees darkness. Releasing negativity frees you to live a life filled with gratitude and love.

TODAY'S ACTION

Take 30 minutes to journal about any negative experiences or emotions still weighing you down. Write them down, acknowledge them, and practice self-compassion as you release them. If it feels right, contact a trusted friend or professional for support. Lean into forgiveness and free yourself from the weight of the past.

TODAY'S AFFIRMATION

I release negativity and open myself to joy and fulfillment.

July 29

FACE YOUR CHALLENGES

"Stand up to your obstacles and do something about them. You will find that they haven't half the strength you think they have."

—NORMAN VINCENT PEALE

Optimism is the foundation of progress. When you see obstacles as challenges to overcome rather than barriers, you open up a path for growth. Each obstacle you face with courage loses its power over you. Our fear of the challenge often holds us back more than the challenge itself. When you face your fears head-on, you'll discover they're not as impossible as they once seemed.

TODAY'S ACTION

Identify a challenge in your life that's been holding you back. Take one direct step to tackle it today, no matter how small. Whether reaching out for support, gathering resources, or making a simple plan, this step will show you you can overcome it.

TODAY'S AFFIRMATION

I face my challenges with courage, knowing they're smaller than they seem.

JAN

FEB

MAR

APR

MAY

JUN

JUL

AUG

SEP

OCT

NOV

DEC

July 30

KNOW YOUR WHY

"He who has a why to live can bear almost any how."

—FRIEDRICH NIETZSCHE

Your purpose is the guiding force behind your choices and actions. The "why" fuels your passion and provides clarity in your life. Knowing your why helps you make decisions that resonate with your core values, creating an aligned, meaningful, and fulfilling life. When you're clear on your purpose, each step you take feels more intentional and connected to your long-term vision.

TODAY'S ACTION

Today, dive deep into discovering your core purpose. Choose a meaningful goal or project, and ask yourself, "Why is this important to me?" Write down your answer, then ask "Why?" again. Keep peeling back the layers with each "Why?" until you uncover the root reason. This exercise clarifies your motivations and reveals the core purpose that drives you.

TODAY'S AFFIRMATION

My choices and actions align with my purpose.

July 31

BE STILL AND PRAY

"Be still, and know that I am God."

—Psalm 46:10

In stillness and prayer, you find peace, guidance, and strength. God's presence becomes clear in those quiet moments, offering wisdom and love. In a world filled with constant noise and endless distractions, choosing silence is almost an act of rebellion—but it's essential. When you quiet your mind, you open your heart to receive. Silence in prayer is not just the absence of sound; it's the presence of God.

TODAY'S ACTION

Set aside a few minutes today for silence and prayer. Find a peaceful spot, close your eyes, and listen to what you most need to hear. Let your heart be still and listen. Trust that the guidance and next steps will come from this calm place.

TODAY'S AFFIRMATION

I invite stillness and peace into my life.

August

August 1

VISUALIZE YOUR FUTURE

"The only person you are destined to become
is the person you decide to be."

—RALPH WALDO EMERSON

Your imagination is a blueprint for the life you desire. By
visualizing your goals, you actively draw them into reality.
When you let yourself truly experience the emotions,
sensations, and joy of having achieved your dream, you
ignite a magnetic energy that brings your vision closer.
This isn't just daydreaming; it's creating clarity and
commitment to the future you want to live.

TODAY'S ACTION

Pick one meaningful goal or dream from your bucket list
and set aside at least 5 minutes to fully immerse yourself
in dreaming about it. Sit in a quiet place, close your eyes,
and picture yourself living that reality. Imagine every
detail—what you see, hear, and feel. If it's owning a home,
visualize walking through it; if it's a career milestone,
imagine celebrating it. Afterward, jot down any thoughts
or emotions that came up during the exercise. Revisit this
visualization regularly to strengthen your commitment.

TODAY'S AFFIRMATION

I bring my dreams closer with each vision I create.

JAN

FEB

MAR

APR

MAY

JUN

JUL

AUG

SEP

OCT

NOV

DEC

August 2

LOVE WHAT YOU DO

"The only way to do great work is to love what you do."

—STEVE JOBS

When you love what you do, even challenging days feel meaningful. Passion fuels purpose. True fulfillment comes from aligning your time and energy with things that bring you positivity and make you feel alive. Loving what you do isn't about every moment being easy—it's about finding purpose and joy in your journey.

TODAY'S ACTION

Identify one task or activity that brings you joy, whether part of your work or something personal. Carve out time for it today, and fully immerse yourself in the experience. Allow this moment to remind you of the importance of passion in your daily life. If you're feeling inspired, consider how you might bring more of what you love into your routine.

TODAY'S AFFIRMATION

I choose to fill my life with work that inspires and fulfills me.

BE TRUE TO YOU

"If you're not being criticized, you're probably not doing much."

—ELON MUSK

Being true to yourself is more powerful than being liked. Positivity isn't about pleasing everyone but the courage to stand by your values, goals, and dreams. When you let go of the need for approval, you free yourself to live with greater authenticity and joy. Choosing self-respect over people-pleasing not only strengthens your confidence but also attracts those who genuinely support your journey.

TODAY'S ACTION

Today, consider a recent decision or opinion that felt true to you but might not please everyone else. Reflect on why it mattered to you and honor your choice without judgment. As a bonus challenge, practice saying "no" today to something that doesn't align with your values. Notice how this small act of self-respect shifts your energy.

TODAY'S AFFIRMATION

I live authentically, honoring my values without seeking approval.

JAN
FEB
MAR
APR
MAY
JUN
JUL
AUG
SEP
OCT
NOV
DEC

August 4

FUEL YOUR PURPOSE

"The more you lose yourself in something bigger than yourself, the more energy you will have."

—NORMAN VINCENT PEALE

Positive energy comes from aligning with a purpose beyond your own needs. When you engage in work or activities that are meaningful and fulfilling, you tap into a source of strength and enthusiasm that goes far beyond physical energy. This alignment fuels you, making even challenges feel more manageable and providing a sense of happiness from within.

TODAY'S ACTION

Identify one goal or vision you have that benefits others or creates a positive ripple. Set aside dedicated time today to make a decisive move on this goal—take one significant action that drives it forward. Do it with complete focus and purpose, whether reaching out to someone, sharing your message publicly, or tackling a step you've been putting off. Feel the strength of investing your energy into something beyond you, and let it fuel your journey toward meaningful impact.

TODAY'S AFFIRMATION

I create positive energy when I serve the world.

STAND FIRM IN YOUR BELIEFS

"One man with courage makes a majority."

—ANDREW JACKSON

True strength comes from standing firm in what you believe. Even if you're standing alone, stay true to yourself. Courage has the power to inspire and create change. When you remain true to your convictions, you embody a quiet strength that others respect and admire. Through this resilience, you build a foundation others can lean on and trust. Remember, courage isn't the absence of fear—it's choosing to act despite it and knowing that staying grounded in your values will always lead you in the right direction.

TODAY'S ACTION

Reflect on a belief or value that you hold close to your heart. Today, take one small action to uphold this value, whether by speaking up, setting a boundary, or following through on something that aligns with your word. Notice how standing firm strengthens your sense of self.

TODAY'S AFFIRMATION

I stand firm in my beliefs and let courage lead my actions.

JAN
FEB
MAR
APR
MAY
JUN
JUL
AUG
SEP
OCT
NOV
DEC

August 6

REFLECT ON YOUR HABITS

"Your life is a reflection of your thoughts. If you change your thinking, you change your life."

—BRIAN TRACY

Every incredible journey is built on small, steady steps.
Like a car slowly moving through traffic, even a little progress brings you closer to your dreams. Research shows that small, consistent actions—those tiny habits—can create powerful, lasting change. Moving forward, however slowly, is still forward.

TODAY'S ACTION

Create a "Habit Tracker" for the next seven days. Write down one small, positive habit aligned with your goals, like drinking more water, reading for 10 minutes, or journaling each morning. Place a checkmark each day you complete it. At the end of the week, reflect on your progress and any shifts you notice. Let this simple tool keep you motivated and build momentum, one day at a time.

TODAY'S AFFIRMATION

I take consistent and deliberate action toward my dreams.

August 7

COUNT YOUR BLESSINGS

"Instead of looking at what's depressing, look at what's a blessing."

—KRISTEN BUTLER

Gratitude shifts your focus from what's wrong to what's strong. Counting your blessings can transform your mindset and bring positivity into your day. Even when life feels challenging, focusing on what's going right can reveal new opportunities and open new doors. Studies show that you train your mind to see the good by counting your blessings, boosting your mental health. It's your time to turn obstacles into opportunities and setbacks into comebacks.

TODAY'S ACTION

List three challenges you're currently facing. For each, write down one potential blessing or silver lining. Then, take one practical step to express gratitude—such as sending a thank-you message, writing in your journal, or offering a quick prayer. This habit will help you transform obstacles into growth opportunities.

TODAY'S AFFIRMATION

I see the silver lining in every challenge.

JAN
FEB
MAR
APR
MAY
JUN
JUL
AUG
SEP
OCT
NOV
DEC

August 8

FIND PURPOSE IN PAIN

"God has a purpose behind the pain."

—BRUCE FRANK

Pain is a pathway to purpose. Pain can feel like an unwelcome guest, yet every struggle holds a deeper purpose. Trusting in God's plan means believing that each challenge has the power to grow, teach, and strengthen us in ways we may not yet understand. Embracing this perspective transforms hardship into an opportunity to deepen your faith and resilience. Remember, your challenges don't define you—they refine you.

TODAY'S ACTION

Reflect on a recent challenge you've faced. Take a moment to pray about how this experience might be shaping you for the better. Can you see areas where it has strengthened your faith, increased your compassion, or built your resilience? Thank God for that. Use this time to ask God for guidance and trust in His purpose.

TODAY'S AFFIRMATION

Every challenge leads me closer to my purpose.

ACTIVATE THE POWER OF PRAYER

"The greatest tragedy of life is not unanswered prayer, but unoffered prayer."

—F.B. Meyer

Your greatest strength lies in the prayers you offer. In the busyness of life, it's easy to try handling everything on your own. The real power comes from inviting God's guidance into our lives. Prayer connects you to the divine—a source of strength, clarity, and peace. When you make prayer your first response, you open the door to the ultimate support and wisdom.

TODAY'S ACTION

Reflect on a time when a prayer brought you comfort, clarity, or protection. Set aside time to pray intentionally. Align your heart with faith and invite God's presence into your challenges and goals. Notice the calm that follows, reminding you that you're supported every step of the way.

TODAY'S AFFIRMATION

I trust in God's guidance and find strength and peace in prayer.

JAN
FEB
MAR
APR
MAY
JUN
JUL
AUG
SEP
OCT
NOV
DEC

August 10

IDENTIFY WHAT'S WORKING

"You don't have to be a genius, visionary, or even a college graduate to succeed. You just need a framework and a dream."

—MICHAEL DELL

Success begins by recognizing what's already working. When you focus on the habits, strategies, and actions bringing you positive results, you amplify their power and impact. Living intentionally means choosing to prioritize and nurture what's practical. You create space for even more growth and success by directing your attention towards thriving.

TODAY'S ACTION

Take a success snapshot. Identify one area of your life where you see positive results—big or small. Write down the habits, actions, and mindsets contributing to this success. Reflect on how you can double down on these strengths by giving them more time and energy. For an added challenge, think about ways to apply this framework to other areas of your life. When you focus on what's working, you build momentum and invite more positivity into your life.

TODAY'S AFFIRMATION

I focus on what's working and allow it to expand.

WELLNESS IS KEY

"Wellness is a journey, not a destination. It's about progress, not perfection."

—Dr. Amy Shah

Your body is your foundation. When you're energized and healthy, everything feels more achievable. But when you're drained or in pain, even small tasks can feel overwhelming. Prioritizing wellness is one of the most powerful ways to fuel your health and happiness. Building supportive habits isn't about perfection—it's about honoring your body in ways that nourish and sustain it.

TODAY'S ACTION

Do a "body check" today. Start with your morning routine: do you begin with movement? Examine your eating habits: are they energizing or weighing you down? Review your exercise—are you giving your muscles, joints, and heart the necessary care? Finally, assess your sleep—are you letting your body rest and recharge? Make one slight adjustment today to support your wellness.

TODAY'S AFFIRMATION

I care for my body and enjoy feeling healthy and happy.

JAN

FEB

MAR

APR

MAY

JUN

JUL

AUG

SEP

OCT

NOV

DEC

August 12

BUILDING SELF-TRUST

"Self-trust is the first secret of success."

—RALPH WALDO EMERSON

Trusting yourself is the foundation of true success.
When you have self-trust, you stop relying on others' opinions to guide you and start relying on your inner wisdom. Self-trust allows you to confidently make choices, knowing you're aligned with your values and true to who you are. With each decision you make from this place of inner trust, you strengthen your resilience and move forward with clarity.

TODAY'S ACTION

Identify one area where you can lean more into self-trust. It could be a decision you've been second-guessing or a goal you've been hesitating to pursue. Write down one small step you can take today to act on your instincts, regardless of outside opinions. Notice how empowering it feels to follow through on what feels right for you.

TODAY'S AFFIRMATION

I trust myself and make decisions that honor my true path.

August 13

VISUALIZE TOMORROW

"You've got to visualize where you're headed and be very clear about it. Take a polaroid picture of where you're going to be in a few years."

—Sarah Blakely

Visualization is the foundation of transformation.
Creating a clear, vivid image of your future activates your brain's ability to turn dreams into reality. Positive affirmations can amplify this process by grounding your vision in confidence and self-belief. Whenever you affirm your worth and capabilities, you build a mindset that propels you forward with optimism and courage.

TODAY'S ACTION

Pick a powerful affirmation that aligns with the future you want to create—something like, "I am capable of achieving my dreams." Throughout the day, repeat this affirmation. Say it in the mirror, jot it in your journal, or set it as a reminder on your phone. Visualize yourself living out this affirmation and feel its truth. Let each repetition bring you closer to the future you envision.

TODAY'S AFFIRMATION

I am moving closer to my goals every day.

August 14

VALUE YOURSELF FIRST

"Your value doesn't decrease based on
someone's inability to see your worth."

—Zig Ziglar

Self-worth is the foundation of a positive life. When you
recognize your value, you stand stronger, face challenges
with resilience, and make choices that align with your
true self. Embracing your worth isn't about external
validation; it's about knowing you are valuable just as
you are. This mindset shapes how you see the world and
how the world responds to you. Remember, the first step
in creating a positive life is understanding and honoring
the value you bring.

TODAY'S ACTION

Take a moment today to affirm your worth. Write down
three specific qualities that make you proud to be you.
Keep them visible as a reminder throughout the day.
In moments of self-doubt or negativity, please return
to this list and let it reinforce your inner strength. Small
reminders like these nurture a powerful, lasting sense of
self-worth.

TODAY'S AFFIRMATION

I honor and embrace my inherent worth, knowing I am
valuable just as I am.

CREATE YOUR ROADMAP

"Plans are nothing; planning is everything."

—Dwight D. Eisenhower

Planning is where dreams meet reality. A plan alone is a starting point, but the process of planning fuels progress. When you take the time to map out each step, you're not only creating a guide—you're preparing yourself to handle challenges. Thoughtful planning brings clarity and structure to your journey, empowering you to adapt as you move forward.

TODAY'S ACTION

Start your success roadmap. Take recent notes on your goals and dreams and begin structuring them into a step-by-step action plan. Prioritize tasks in order of importance, set deadlines, and identify any resources you'll need. Add a column for potential obstacles, and brainstorm solutions to stay proactive. Each step you outline today brings you closer to realizing your goals.

TODAY'S AFFIRMATION

I invest time in planning to turn my goals into reality.

JAN

FEB

MAR

APR

MAY

JUN

JUL

AUG

SEP

OCT

NOV

DEC

August 16

UNLOCK YOUR POTENTIAL

"The unexamined life is not worth living."

—SOCRATES

Real discovery begins within. You unlock strengths, hidden beauty, and untapped potential by looking at yourself with fresh eyes. This shift in perspective can be life-changing, showing you that the qualities you need to succeed and grow are already within you. Each new insight is an invitation to see yourself as you are—unique, capable, and full of possibility. Embrace this vision, and let it guide you to a life of positivity!

TODAY'S ACTION

Take 30 minutes today for self-reflection. Identify a quality or strength within that you may have overlooked. Journal on how developing this part of yourself could add depth and purpose to your journey. Keep this discovery close to your heart, and let it fuel your confidence as you move forward.

TODAY'S AFFIRMATION

I see and celebrate the best in myself and grow every day.

August 17

SIMPLIFY FOR SUCCESS

"The secret to productivity is simplicity."

—MEL ROBBINS

Simplicity fuels success. When you strip away the clutter and focus on what truly matters, each step becomes clearer, stronger, and more intentional. Streamlining your actions isn't just about doing less—it's about doing what counts. Cutting out distractions and unnecessary steps opens up space for real progress. Productivity thrives when you commit to clarity and purpose, turning big goals into doable actions that move you forward.

TODAY'S ACTION

Take the 3-Item challenge today. Choose three essential tasks that will push you closer to your goal and make them your sole focus. Break each task down to its simplest form, removing anything nonessential. Forget the "nice-to-haves" and zero in on what truly matters. Reflect on how this focus brought momentum and clarity to your progress.

TODAY'S AFFIRMATION

I clear the path to my goals by focusing on what matters most.

JAN

FEB

MAR

APR

MAY

JUN

JUL

AUG

SEP

OCT

NOV

DEC

August 18

SET YOUR MILESTONES

"A goal is a dream with a deadline."

—Napoleon Hill

Small wins build significant momentum. Like the dopamine rush from checking your phone, achieving milestones motivates your brain. No matter how small, each accomplishment boosts your drive to keep moving forward. Setting clear milestones creates a positive feedback loop of progress and reward that brings your dreams within reach. All you have to do to achieve them is keep going!

TODAY'S ACTION

Break down one of your big goals into three small, achievable milestones. Write them down and set a target date for each. Celebrate each step as you reach it— acknowledging your progress keeps the momentum and fuels your commitment. Reward yourself in a small way after finishing all three. Then, set three more to keep the momentum flowing.

TODAY'S AFFIRMATION

I celebrate each step forward as I move steadily toward my dreams.

August 19

RESET TO RECHARGE

"Almost everything will work again if you unplug it for a few minutes, including you."

—ANNE LAMOTT

Stepping back can be the most powerful way to move forward. Breaks aren't just pauses; they're mini reboots that clear your mind, lift your energy, and refresh your focus. When you take a few moments to unplug, you return to your tasks with more clarity, creativity, and purpose. By embracing rest, you create space for calm and invite space for positivity into your day.

TODAY'S ACTION

Set a timer for every hour today, or as often as possible, as a reminder to pause and reset. During each 5-minute break, step outside if possible, take a few deep breaths, or stretch gently. Let this be a time to recharge and refocus, allowing yourself to return to your tasks with fresh energy and calm.

TODAY'S AFFIRMATION

I honor my need for rest, knowing it fuels my peace and productivity.

JAN

FEB

MAR

APR

MAY

JUN

JUL

AUG

SEP

OCT

NOV

DEC

August 20

STEP INTO COURAGE

"Courage is the essence of character. It's what sets the extraordinary apart from the ordinary."

—Lauren Magers

Courage is what transforms ordinary moments into defining ones. It's not the absence of fear but the decision to act in the face of it. True strength comes from stepping into discomfort, knowing it leads to growth, and trusting that avoiding it builds more discomfort over time. Each time you act with courage, you honor your character and move closer to the person you're meant to become.

TODAY'S ACTION

Choose one conversation you've been putting off and commit to having it today. Approach it with an open heart. Take a few deep, grounding breaths. Center yourself in compassion and love. Leading with courage is about healing, growth, and creating stronger connections. Trust this brave leap forward.

TODAY'S AFFIRMATION

I approach difficult conversations with courage and an open heart.

August 21

BE KIND TO YOUR MIND

"Be kind to yourself, it's the best medicine to heal and grow."

—Aziz Farheen

Letting go of self-judgment is a powerful act of self-care. When was the last time you looked in the mirror and thought, "Wow! I am beautiful just as I am"? Or completed a task and said, "I'm proud of you for doing that so well"? We reserve praise and kindness for others while giving ourselves only criticism and judgment. By releasing harsh self-criticism, you reduce anxiety, build confidence, and open yourself to growth.

TODAY'S ACTION

Pay close attention to your self-talk today. When judgmental or critical thoughts arise, acknowledge them, then let them go. Challenge yourself to respond with kindness and positivity instead. Notice the impact it has on your mood and mindset when you choose self-compassion over self-criticism.

TODAY'S AFFIRMATION

I embrace my strengths and uniqueness with kindness.

JAN

FEB

MAR

APR

MAY

JUN

JUL

AUG

SEP

OCT

NOV

DEC

August 22

SWEAT WITH STRENGTH

"Sweat is just fat crying."

—Jillian Michaels

Every drop of sweat is proof of your strength. When you commit to cardio, you're giving your heart the workout it deserves, and each drop of sweat tells the story of your resilience. Sweating through exercise isn't just about fitness. It's a powerful way to release stress, boost your mood, and remind yourself that you can do great things. Harness the energy of moving your body, and let each step strengthen your heart and spirit.

TODAY'S ACTION

Challenge yourself to a cardio workout that makes you sweat. Choose an activity you enjoy—a run, jump rope session, or upbeat dance workout—and set a goal to keep your heart rate up for 20 minutes. As you feel the sweat, let it remind you of the strength you're building from the inside out. Remember, cardio isn't just about burning calories—it's about strengthening the organ that gives you life.

TODAY'S AFFIRMATION

I sweat with strength and build a healthier heart each day.

August 23

RELEASE & RENEW

"Muscle relaxation is not a luxury; it's a necessity. It's what allows us to unwind, recharge, and face life's challenges with renewed energy."

—ARIANNA HUFFINGTON

Letting go of muscle tension is a gift to both body and mind. Many of us carry stress in our bodies without even realizing it. When you consciously relax your muscles, you invite a sense of calm and create space for clarity. Easing physical tension recharges your body, lifts your spirit, and brings peace to your mind.

TODAY'S ACTION

Find a comfortable place to sit or lie down, close your eyes, and take a deep breath. Slowly work down your body from your forehead, relaxing each muscle group. Focus on releasing tension in your face, neck, shoulders, and toes. With each exhale, let go of any tightness you feel. Return to this simple practice whenever you need a moment of calm.

TODAY'S AFFIRMATION

As I release the tension in my body, I create space for peace and positivity.

JAN
FEB
MAR
APR
MAY
JUN
JUL
AUG
SEP
OCT
NOV
DEC

August 24

TRUST THE PROCESS

"When you trust the process, the journey
becomes as rewarding as the destination."

—KRISTEN BUTLER

Trusting the process is a powerful act of faith. Life's path
can be unpredictable, with twists that challenge us and
turns that surprise us. When we let go of the need to control
every outcome, we open ourselves to growth, resilience,
and unexpected blessings. This mindset can allow doors
to open and opportunities to start flowing in. Embracing
each step with trust brings peace, purpose, and positivity,
allowing us to enjoy the journey as it unfolds.

TODAY'S ACTION

Grab a sheet of paper and write "Trust the Process" at
the top. Create two columns labeled "Challenge" and
"Blessing."In the "Challenge" column, jot down an area of
uncertainty or impatience. In the "Blessing" column, list
any positive lessons, growth, or connections this journey
has brought you or will bring you when you are on the
other side. Let this be a reminder that each step holds
meaning and purpose, even if it's hard to see right now.

TODAY'S AFFIRMATION

I trust the process and enjoy the journey.

LEAD WITH INTEGRITY

"Whatever you are, be a good one."

—ABRAHAM LINCOLN

Integrity is your strongest foundation. The internal compass guides you to act in alignment with your values, even when no one's watching. When you lead with integrity, you build a life of honesty, trust, and respect. Integrity deepens self-respect and naturally earns the respect of others. Staying true to your principles brings peace and fulfillment that nothing else can replace.

TODAY'S ACTION

Identify one area of your life where you can show up with more integrity. Consider a habit, promise, or boundary you could uphold more consistently. Take one specific action today—complete a postponed task, have an honest conversation, or set a new boundary. Each act of integrity strengthens your foundation of trust with yourself and others.

TODAY'S AFFIRMATION

I live with integrity, staying true to my values in every action.

JAN
FEB
MAR
APR
MAY
JUN
JUL
AUG
SEP
OCT
NOV
DEC

August 26

RADIATE POSITIVITY

"Whatever is true, noble, right, pure, lovely, admirable—if anything is excellent or praiseworthy—think about such things."

—PHILIPPIANS 4:8

Positivity flows from a heart focused on what's good and true. When you intentionally direct your thoughts toward what's pure and admirable, you cultivate a spirit that radiates light to others. Every action, word, and thought can reflect excellence and grace, creating a ripple effect that brightens your world and inspires those around you.

TODAY'S ACTION

Take the "Radiate Positivity Challenge." Throughout your day, embody true, noble, and praiseworthy qualities. In each interaction, choose words and actions that reflect integrity and kindness. Make a habit of checking in with yourself to ensure your thoughts and actions align with these values, letting this mindset become part of who you are.

TODAY'S AFFIRMATION

I embody positivity, integrity, and light in all I do daily.

August 27

START WITH SUCCESS

"If you want to change the world, start off by making your bed."

—WILLIAM H. MCRAVEN

Small actions can have a big impact. Making your bed may seem minor, but it sets the tone for a productive day. This simple task is your first win, giving you a sense of accomplishment and control. When you start with order and intention, you create a ripple effect that supports more focused, successful days.

TODAY'S ACTION

If you still need to, make your bed! Then, for the rest of the week, commit to making it as soon as you wake up. Notice how this small action influences your mindset, energy, and productivity. Want an extra boost? Download our free guide at riseandshineon.com to fuel your morning routine and carry this momentum throughout the day.

TODAY'S AFFIRMATION

I take small, intentional actions that set me up for success.

JAN

FEB

MAR

APR

MAY

JUN

JUL

AUG

SEP

OCT

NOV

DEC

August 28

OWN YOUR ACTIONS

"A leader who doesn't take accountability for their actions is like a ship without a captain."

—John C. Maxwell

Accountability is the anchor of authentic leadership.
Taking ownership of your actions is what moves you forward. When you take responsibility for your actions, you steer your life purposefully. It's not just about going through the motions—it's about committing to what matters most and owning your journey. Without accountability, even the best intentions drift off course. But with it, every step aligns with your goals and confidently moves you forward.

TODAY'S ACTION

Today, transform your to-do list into a powerful tool for progress. Go through each task one by one. First, decide if it's essential—if not, let it go. If it is, determine if it's something you must handle or can be delegated. For what remains, assign a specific time and duration to each task and add it to your calendar. This focused approach will help you prioritize effectively, streamline your actions, and eliminate overwhelm.

TODAY'S AFFIRMATION

I take ownership of my time, focusing only on what matters most.

August 29

UNCOVER YOUR PROCRASTINATION

"You are not stuck where you are unless you decide to be."

—WAYNE DYER

Procrastination often hides an important message. It can signal that something feels overwhelming, unclear, or unaligned with your values. Maybe you're hesitating because of a fear of failure, or the task feels unimportant or confusing. Instead of ignoring or criticizing your hesitation, could you take a moment to understand it? Procrastination doesn't mean laziness. It's your intuition nudging you to pause and reflect.

TODAY'S ACTION

Choose one task you've been putting off and take a deeper look. What's holding you back—fear, confusion, lack of interest, or something else? Once you identify the root cause, address it directly: simplify the task, seek support, or adjust your approach. Set a small, achievable goal to create momentum and take one step toward completion today.

TODAY'S AFFIRMATION

I honor my needs and take intentional steps forward.

JAN
FEB
MAR
APR
MAY
JUN
JUL
AUG
SEP
OCT
NOV
DEC

August 30

CHOOSE TO SEE THE GOOD

"Find the good. It's all around you. Find it, showcase it, and you'll start believing in it."

—Jesse Owens

Your perspective shapes your reality. By seeing the good in each moment, you train your mind to find positivity even in challenging times. This doesn't mean ignoring difficulties but rather focusing on the growth, lessons, and small joys within them. A positive outlook empowers you to handle obstacles with strength, resilience, and hope, knowing that each day holds something to be grateful for.

TODAY'S ACTION

Create a "Gratitude Chain" today. Begin by writing down one positive thing that happened in the last 24 hours on paper or your journal. Then, let this thought lead you to another related positive moment, and write that down, too. Keep linking moments, allowing each one to remind you of another good thing in your life. By the end of the chain, you'll have a collection of positive reflections that uplift and energize you.

TODAY'S AFFIRMATION

I focus on the good in each moment, attracting more positivity and joy.

August 31

DO WHAT YOU CAN

"Do what you can with all you have, wherever you are."

—THEODORE ROOSEVELT

Progress is built in small, steady steps. It's not about waiting for ideal conditions or perfect timing—it's about doing what you can with what you have today. Each action, no matter how small, moves you forward. When you take even one step, you tell yourself, "I am committed." Over time, these actions gather momentum, pushing you closer to your dreams.

TODAY'S ACTION

Choose one simple but meaningful action that supports your goals today. Take this step with intention, whether a single email, a five-minute reflection, or reaching out for support. As you go about your day, acknowledge each small accomplishment by saying, "Good job." Celebrate these wins, knowing they're building a solid foundation for what's next. Let today's small steps be the start of something powerful.

TODAY'S AFFIRMATION

I celebrate each step forward as I move closer to my dreams.

September

September 1

LIVE WITH INTENTION

"Living with intention means saying no to the things that aren't aligned with your highest values and purpose."

—Brendon Burchard

Intentions turn dreams into direction. Without them, life feels like driving without a destination—aimless and unfocused. You're in the driver's seat when you set intentional goals, steering your life with purpose and clarity. Each day becomes a step toward a more meaningful, fulfilling life. Living intentionally isn't just about setting goals—it's about aligning each choice with your core values and highest purpose.

TODAY'S ACTION

Begin and end your day with clear intentions. This morning, choose three things you want to accomplish or experience. Write them down as reminders of your focus. Tonight, reflect on your progress and set intentions for tomorrow. With each step, you're creating a purposeful life, one day at a time.

TODAY'S AFFIRMATION

I live each day with clear intentions and purpose.

September 2

KEEP GOING STRONG

"Even if you're on the right track, you'll
get run over if you just sit there."

—WILL ROGERS

Taking action is what turns plans into progress. Moving forward is about more than being on the right path. It's about taking the next step. Progress comes from consistent, intentional action, no matter how small. Waiting around for the "perfect moment" can leave you stuck. When you take the most straightforward action, you create energy and build momentum that fuels your day. Every small win pushes you further, turning intention into progress.

TODAY'S ACTION

Look at your to-do list and choose the most straightforward task. Complete it first thing in the morning and allow yourself a moment to celebrate this small win. Notice how it shifts your energy and sets a positive tone for the day. As you progress, let each small accomplishment build confidence and open the door to tackling more significant tasks.

TODAY'S AFFIRMATION

Each small step builds my momentum and drives me forward.

September 3

LET LOVE TRANSFORM

"Love is the only force capable of transforming an enemy into a friend."

—Martin Luther King Jr.

Love changes everything. It's the energy that can heal wounds, dissolve resentment, and bridge divides. Choosing love over anger or judgment creates space for compassion, connection, and understanding. True transformation starts with love—the foundation for peace, growth, and resilience.

TODAY'S ACTION

Today, let love be your guiding force. Choose one person with whom you've felt tension or distance and take a step toward connection. Send them a message of kindness or gratitude, or do something that expresses your appreciation without expecting anything in return. Let this act of love transform both your perspective and your relationship.

TODAY'S AFFIRMATION

I let love guide my actions, creating peace and connection in every area of my life.

JAN
FEB
MAR
APR
MAY
JUN
JUL
AUG
SEP
OCT
NOV
DEC

September 4

CHOOSE TO SHINE

"Keep your face to the sun, and you will never see the shadows."

—HELEN KELLER

When we choose to shine, we align with hope and strength. Shadows lose their power, and light fills the space. Standing in the sunlight isn't just about warmth and positive vibes. It's about letting go of what weighs us down and inviting in what lifts us up. The sun is a reminder of our inner light—a light that heals, empowers, and connects us to peace. Each moment we spend facing the light is a moment we choose resilience over worry, faith over fear.

TODAY'S ACTION

Spend ten to fifteen minutes outside in the morning sun. If possible, stand barefoot on grass, sand, or soil. Walk, stretch out on the grass, or settle under a tree. As you breathe deeply, feel the sun's warmth filling you. Imagine a calm, steady light glowing within your heart, expanding with each breath to surround your entire being. Let this natural light fill you up and allow you to shine from within.

TODAY'S AFFIRMATION

I choose light, letting peace and strength fill me.

UNLEASH YOUR POTENTIAL

"Your greatest power is knowing you haven't even scratched the surface of what you're capable of."

—ED MYLETT

Within you lies everything you need to shine. Imagine if today you tapped into just a little more of your potential— what might you achieve? Each day is an opportunity to stretch further, expand your comfort zone, and unleash your potential. The more you believe in what you're capable of, the more you'll uncover strengths you didn't know you had. Trust that within you lies everything you need.

TODAY'S ACTION

Challenge yourself today to do one thing that stretches your comfort zone. It might be having a tough conversation, setting a boundary, or trying something new. Whatever it is, approach it with confidence, knowing it's a step toward your best life. Afterward, take a moment to reflect on how this made you feel. Celebrate your effort, and recognize that each challenge brings you closer to the best version of yourself.

TODAY'S AFFIRMATION

I am constantly evolving, unlocking the greatness within me.

JAN
FEB
MAR
APR
MAY
JUN
JUL
AUG
SEP
OCT
NOV
DEC

September 6

RELAX, RELEASE, RECHARGE

"Sometimes the most productive thing you can do is relax."

—MARK BLACK

Relaxation is more than a luxury—it's essential. A calm and balanced nervous system creates the foundation for health, resilience, and mental clarity. Studies show that moments of genuine relaxation release tension, sharpen focus, and uplift our overall well-being. Choosing to relax isn't stepping away from productivity; it's setting ourselves up for more profound health, happiness, and growth. Treat relaxation as an investment in yourself.

TODAY'S ACTION

Schedule a massage this week. Whether it's a spa treatment or a soothing back rub with your partner, let this be a gift to yourself. If a massage isn't an option, find a way to release tension today. Try using a pressure point ball, a foam roller, or a relaxing Pilates class. Each moment you relax, you're inviting in more peace and energy. Let today mark the beginning of a relaxation ritual that recharges you.

TODAY'S AFFIRMATION

I am worthy of rest, relaxation, and renewal.

FOCUS TO FLOURISH

"What you stay focused on will grow."

—Roy T. Bennett

Your focus is powerful—what you give attention to, you nourish. Life expands when you consistently focus on positive thoughts, goals, and actions. This is how you create momentum in life. Just like a garden, what you tend to will flourish. By focusing on growth, gratitude, and positivity, you're setting yourself up for lasting change. Remember, energy flows where attention goes, so choose wisely and watch your intentions blossom.

TODAY'S ACTION

Take a few minutes to reflect on one goal or positive habit you'd like to grow. Write it down somewhere you'll see it daily—on a sticky note, journal, or as a reminder on your phone. Commit to focusing on this for the next week. Each day, spend a few moments visualizing this intention coming to life and take one small action toward it.

TODAY'S AFFIRMATION

My focus brings growth, positivity, and change.

September 8

MASTER YOUR MINDSET

"Your thoughts shape your reality. When you
master your mindset, you master your life."

—Kristen Butler

Your mindset is the foundation for everything. A
positive mindset improves mental well-being, physical
health, and overall success. It's about choosing to see
challenges as opportunities, setbacks as lessons, and
every day as a chance to grow. When you start your day
by mastering your mindset, you set the tone for how you
will navigate life. It's not about avoiding negativity but
directing your thoughts toward growth, gratitude, and
possibility.

TODAY'S ACTION

Begin your day with a mindset check. Before diving into
your tasks, take a moment to set a positive intention.
Choose one uplifting thought or affirmation to carry with
you, and when negativity arises, consciously replace it
with your chosen thought. This simple practice helps
keep you focused, motivated, and resilient throughout
the day.

TODAY'S AFFIRMATION

I choose thoughts that bring positivity and strength.

FIND SIMPLICITY

"Out of clutter, find simplicity."

—ALBERT EINSTEIN

Simplicity creates space for what truly matters. Clutter clouds not just our spaces but also our minds. Embracing simplicity helps us see what truly matters, freeing us from the distractions that weigh us down. When we let go of what we no longer need, we create space for clarity, calm, purpose, and positivity. Simplifying our surroundings reminds us to prioritize what supports and nourishes us.

TODAY'S ACTION

Choose one area of your home to organize today, such as a drawer, closet, or shelf. Remove everything, discard what no longer serves you, and mindfully arrange what you decide to keep. This small act of clearing and organizing creates a sense of calm and order, leaving you feeling lighter and more intentional in your surroundings.

TODAY'S AFFIRMATION

I am worthy of health, simplicity, and a positive life.

September 10

POSITIVE BODY LANGUAGE

"The body language you use when you're in a positive mood can affect your mindset, and can even have an impact on the people around you."

—AMY CUDDY

How you carry yourself affects how you feel—and how others feel around you. When you stand tall, you send a message of strength and confidence. Open posture invites positivity and energizes you from within. Simple shifts in how you stand can spark powerful changes in your mindset. Creating openness in your body sets the stage for a brighter, bolder day.

TODAY'S ACTION

Practice open body language today. Before any meeting, interaction, or moment to yourself, lift your gaze, breathe deeply, sit tall, and relax your shoulders. Feel the shift. Let this simple act fill you with optimism and resilience. Consider being more intentional about your body language daily to invite positive energy.

TODAY'S AFFIRMATION

I stand tall with open and positive body language.

September 11

HONOR FREEDOM WITH UNITY

"Freedom is never more than one generation away from extinction."

—RONALD REAGAN

Freedom is both a privilege and a responsibility. It's a legacy passed down by those who sacrificed and stood firm in times of trial. Today, we're reminded that freedom unites us and calls us to uplift each other. In moments of darkness, our greatest strength has always been our ability to unite. True freedom means standing as one, honoring our differences, and lifting each other.

TODAY'S ACTION

Take a moment today to connect with someone in your community. Reach out with a message of kindness or gratitude, or lend a helping hand. Consider volunteering, donating, or simply listening to someone's story. Let your actions reflect the unity that makes freedom possible and the strength that unites us.

TODAY'S AFFIRMATION

I honor freedom by showing compassion, unity, and resilience in my community.

JAN

FEB

MAR

APR

MAY

JUN

JUL

AUG

SEP

OCT

NOV

DEC

September 12

PRAY FOR STRENGTH

"I know God won't give me anything I can't handle.
I just wish he didn't trust me so much."

—MOTHER TERESA

When life feels overwhelming, prayer becomes a powerful lifeline. It directly connects to a loving God who believes in your resilience. Praying for strength invites support, helping lift the weight of your struggles, and opening your heart to trust in God's guidance. This act of surrender fills you with peace and optimism, reminding you that you're never alone in your challenges.

TODAY'S ACTION

Today, recite the Serenity Prayer: "God, grant me the serenity to accept the things I cannot change, courage to change the things I can, and wisdom to know the difference." Allow these words to center you, renewing your trust in God and your resilience to forge ahead. Feel the peace of being divinely supported.

TODAY'S AFFIRMATION

I am guided and strengthened by God, trusting fully in my resilience.

FOCUS ON IMPACT

"Focus on being productive instead of busy."

—TIM FERRISS

Busy doesn't always mean progress. It's easy to fill a day with tasks and feel like you're going in circles. Actual productivity is intentionally channeling your energy into actions that genuinely move you closer to your goals. Small, focused steps lead to big success. Remember, it's not about doing more; it's about doing what matters most.

TODAY'S ACTION

Choose one high-impact action today that advances a goal that lights you up. Commit fully. Set a timer, eliminate distractions, and give it your best energy. When you're done, take a moment to acknowledge the progress you've created. Share your success with someone who supports you, and commit to keeping this momentum going.

TODAY'S AFFIRMATION

I direct my energy toward actions that create a positive impact.

JAN

FEB

MAR

APR

MAY

JUN

JUL

AUG

SEP

OCT

NOV

DEC

September 14

LOVE YOURSELF OUT LOUD

"Loving yourself isn't vanity; it's sanity."

—KATRINA MAYER

Love isn't a luxury; it's a necessity. Yes, even for yourself. It's easy to get caught up in responsibilities, putting everyone else first, and forgetting about the most important person in your life: you! But when you prioritize your happiness, it creates a ripple effect that makes everything else brighter. Today is your chance to celebrate yourself guilt-free and do something that brings you joy. Embracing self-love means giving yourself the care, kindness, and appreciation you deserve without holding back.

TODAY'S ACTION

What would you do today if it was all about you? Take yourself on a date, even if it's as simple as grabbing your favorite treat, enjoying a peaceful walk, or diving into a hobby you love. Write down a list of your favorite things and pick one to treat yourself to today. And if guilt sneaks in, remind yourself: you deserve to be happy, and taking care of yourself isn't just okay—it's essential.

TODAY'S AFFIRMATION

I am worthy of love, joy, and doing what makes me happy.

September 15

SEE THE LIGHT WITHIN

"Nothing can dim the light which shines from within."

—Maya Angelou

Your inner light is a source of strength, peace, and positivity. In every challenge, there's an opportunity to let this light shine brighter. The more you seek the silver linings in life, the stronger and more radiant your light becomes. This isn't about ignoring hardships—it's about choosing to see how even difficult moments can shape you for the better. When you let your light guide you, you bring hope and love into the world.

TODAY'S ACTION

Take the "Shine Your Light" challenge. Choose one intentional action today that spreads positivity and hope to someone else. It could be a genuine compliment, an offer of help, or even a handwritten note of encouragement. Let your action remind you of the light within you, and notice how sharing it strengthens your resilience and optimism. Let this act be a reminder that your light cannot be dimmed. Shine on!

TODAY'S AFFIRMATION

My light grows stronger with every challenge, guiding me and shining hope into the world.

LISTEN TO YOUR INNER VOICE

"Do not let the noise of others' opinions drown out your inner voice."

—STEVE JOBS

Your inner voice is your guide. In a world of opinions, staying true to yourself is a bold act of courage. The most meaningful decisions come from that deep place within, where intuition and divine guidance align with your values and dreams. Trust that voice—it's there to lead you on the right path, not just the one that appears correct.

TODAY'S ACTION

Find a quiet moment today to tune into your inner voice. Close your eyes, take a few calming breaths, and think about a decision or area of life where you feel uncertain. Listen closely to your gut feeling, free from the influence of others' opinions. Jot down any insights that come to mind and honor the emerging wisdom.

TODAY'S AFFIRMATION

I trust my inner voice and let it guide my journey with confidence and clarity.

JAN FEB MAR APR MAY JUN JUL AUG SEP OCT NOV DEC

September 17

PRIORITIZE POSITIVE RELATIONSHIPS

"The friends that leave you feeling more alive after you're with them are magic in human form."

—Cory Allen

True friends are rare treasures. They make you feel seen, inspired, and alive. Life may pull you in different directions, but nurturing these connections is always worth it. Protect the friends who uplift you—celebrate them, honor them, and let them fuel your best life. Prioritizing positive relationships fills your life with support and a reminder that you are never alone.

TODAY'S ACTION

Pick one friend who brings positivity into your life and reach out to let them know how grateful you are. Set up a time to reconnect—coffee, a call, or a fun event. Celebrate the magic of this friendship by being fully present.

TODAY'S AFFIRMATION

I cherish and honor the people who bring joy and positivity to my life.

JAN

FEB

MAR

APR

MAY

JUN

JUL

AUG

SEP

OCT

NOV

DEC

September 18

KEEP FAITH IN THE JOURNEY

"God never said that the journey would be easy, but
He did say that the arrival would be worthwhile."

—Max Lucado

Every challenge is part of your path. Obstacles aren't setbacks—they're stepping stones. Each step, no matter how tough, builds resilience and draws you closer to the life you're meant to live. Embracing the highs and lows prepares you for the destination. Trust that where you're headed is worth every step you take.

TODAY'S ACTION

Identify one challenge you're currently facing and take a step that moves you forward. It might be seeking advice, trying a new approach, or dedicating focused time to a task you've been avoiding. Think of it as an investment in the "worthwhile arrival" that awaits.

TODAY'S AFFIRMATION

Every step I take brings me closer to a meaningful destination.

September 19

STRENGTH THROUGH SUPPORT

"Ask for help not because you are weak, but because you want to remain strong."

—LES BROWN

Asking for help is a strength, not a weakness. When you reach out, you invite trust, deepen connections, and allow others to show up for you. Think about it—when a friend leans on you, you don't see them as needy; you see them as someone who values your support. In the same way, asking for help gives others the chance to support you. It's a powerful way to nurture relationships, showing love and trust to those who care about you.

TODAY'S ACTION

Choose one task or goal you've been handling alone. Contact a friend, mentor, or family member for specific help. Whether it's advice, a second set of eyes, or even a listening ear, take action and connect with someone today. Let this remind you that seeking support strengthens you and those around you.

TODAY'S AFFIRMATION

I am strong enough to seek support when I need it.

JAN
FEB
MAR
APR
MAY
JUN
JUL
AUG
SEP
OCT
NOV
DEC

September 20

SUCCESS THROUGH JOY

"Success is not the key to happiness. Happiness is the key to success. If you love what you are doing, you will be successful."

—ALBERT SCHWEITZER

True success starts from within. When you love what you're doing, you bring passion, joy, and energy into each moment—and success follows naturally. Happiness fuels progress, turning each step into something to celebrate. By choosing joy in your journey, you create a magnetic pull toward all that you desire—transforming your dreams into reality.

TODAY'S ACTION

Reflect on a recent win you still need to celebrate. Please take a few minutes today to truly honor it. Tell a friend, treat yourself to something special, write about it in your journal, or look in the mirror and acknowledge your pride. Celebrating your wins uplifts your spirit and energizes you to keep going.

TODAY'S AFFIRMATION

I choose joy in my journey and celebrate every step forward.

September 21

SHARE YOUR STORY

"With every beat of the drum, I find my voice and share my story with the world."

—ELEC SIMON

Every story has a rhythm, a beat that is uniquely its own. When you find the courage to share your story, you honor your journey and give others permission to embrace theirs. Stories are powerful—they connect, inspire, and remind us that we're not alone. Each time you share a part of yourself, you light the way for others to find their voice. Your story has power; sharing it is a gift to the world.

TODAY'S ACTION

Seek out an inspiring story today. Listen to a podcast, watch a TED talk, or read a book about someone who has overcome incredible odds. Let their story motivate you and connect with your resilience, courage, and hope. If you feel inspired, take time to journal about your own story. Writing is the first and most powerful step in sharing it with others.

TODAY'S AFFIRMATION

I am inspired and uplifted by the stories of others.

JAN
FEB
MAR
APR
MAY
JUN
JUL
AUG
SEP
OCT
NOV
DEC

September 22

SPEAK INTO YOUR SUCCESS

"Speak positive words into your life every single morning.
Always start the day with positive energy. You deserve it."

—LUKE CHELBOWICZ

**What you visualize and speak about shapes your
reality.** When you vividly picture yourself achieving your
goals, you create a magnetic pull toward that success.
Visualization taps into your inner strength and channels
your energy toward what you desire. But visualization
alone isn't enough. Speaking your goals aloud gives
them life and momentum, aligning your mind, words, and
actions. The magic happens when you think, speak, and
act out positive energy toward your dreams.

TODAY'S ACTION

Take a few minutes today to visualize your success.
Close your eyes and imagine reaching a specific goal
in vivid detail. Feel the emotions, see the outcome, and
immerse yourself in this vision. The clearer and more
energizing your visualization, the more you'll attract
the opportunities and inspiration needed to make it a
reality. Then, speak it into existence—share your vision
with someone else or say it aloud. Feel the power of your
words fueling your commitment.

TODAY'S AFFIRMATION

I visualize and speak my success into reality with clarity
and purpose.

September 23

THRIVE IN YOUR COMFORT ZONE

"When you reach your goals, you should feel energized, even exhilarated, not exhausted and burned out."

—KRISTEN BUTLER

Your Comfort Zone isn't a static place—it's a space that grows and evolves with you. Far from limiting, it's where your strengths, passions, and confidence come alive. Think of it as a foundation to build on what feels natural and empowering. Embracing your Comfort Zone means honoring what makes you feel strong and capable, not pushing yourself to exhaustion. Growth doesn't require stepping out of your comfort zone; it thrives when you stretch and expand within it, using support to reach new levels while staying grounded in who you are.

TODAY'S ACTION

Today, see your Comfort Zone as a source of growth and strength. Reflect on these questions: "What do I truly enjoy? What activities leave me feeling energized and fulfilled? Where do my natural talents shine?" When you focus on what lights you up, you create a life aligned with your strengths. If something feels beyond reach, seek guidance or support to stretch your zone rather than abandoning it altogether.

TODAY'S AFFIRMATION

I expand and thrive within my Comfort Zone.

JAN
FEB
MAR
APR
MAY
JUN
JUL
AUG
SEP
OCT
NOV
DEC

September 24

RECHARGE IN NATURE

"Look deep into nature, and then you will understand everything better."

—Albert Einstein

Nature offers us a powerful space for restoration and clarity. Stepping into a green space doesn't just relax the body—it clears the mind and refreshes the spirit. Studies show that time in nature boosts our immune system, reduces stress, and enhances focus and creativity. Nature's steady rhythms remind us to slow down, find balance, and be.

TODAY'S ACTION

Take a break from the hustle and visit a nearby park, garden, forest, or outdoor space. Spend at least twenty minutes connecting with the natural surroundings. Engage your senses fully—notice the colors, sounds, smells, and textures around you. Breathe deeply and let the fresh air ground and recharge you. Leave your phone behind to savor this moment of peace.

TODAY'S AFFIRMATION

I draw strength and clarity from nature's peace.

SAVOR THE MOMENT

"Be happy in the moment, that's enough. Each moment is all we need, not more."

—Mother Teresa

When you genuinely savor a moment, you connect deeply with life's joy. Savoring brings you fully into the present—immersed in the sights, sounds, tastes, and feelings of now. It's a gentle reminder that happiness isn't something we chase. It's something we can choose right here. When you savor life, each moment becomes an experience to treasure.

TODAY'S ACTION

Pick a simple activity today that you can fully savor. It might be a meal, a walk, a conversation, or resting. Sink into the experience, letting yourself be completely present. Appreciate each detail and let the moment fill you with joy. By savoring these moments, you build a reserve of positive emotions that can lift you when times are tough. This practice strengthens your "happiness muscles" and makes you feel joy daily.

TODAY'S AFFIRMATION

I embrace happiness in each moment, savoring life fully.

JAN

FEB

MAR

APR

MAY

JUN

JUL

AUG

SEP

OCT

NOV

DEC

September 26

ROOTED IN STRENGTH

"A strong lower body is essential for overall strength and stability."

—Serena Williams

A strong foundation keeps you steady and grounded.
You're as young as your legs are strong. A powerful lower body forms the foundation for a positive, active life. Healthy legs support your freedom, balance, and resilience, keeping you grounded and steady. When your legs are powerful, they help you to stand tall, move confidently, and stay resilient through every stage of life.

TODAY'S ACTION

Incorporate squats into your routine today. Regular squats don't just build muscle—they boost your energy, metabolism, and overall vitality. This simple move strengthens your quadriceps, hamstrings, glutes, and core. Aim for a set of 10–15 squats. Feel how each rep supports your strength and mobility. Start with bodyweight, or add dumbbells for an extra challenge. Let today be a step toward a stronger, healthier future.

TODAY'S AFFIRMATION

My strong legs are a powerful tool for lifelong positivity and vitality.

LEARN FROM HONEST FEEDBACK

"Pay attention to negative feedback and solicit it, particularly from friends. Hardly anyone does that, and it's incredibly helpful."

—ELON MUSK

Growth requires a willingness to learn from honest feedback. It's tempting to avoid criticism, but constructive feedback, especially from trusted friends, can be a powerful tool for improvement. Seeking out this kind of feedback shows strength and a commitment to growth. When you're open to different perspectives, you gain valuable insights that help you refine your actions and elevate your potential.

TODAY'S ACTION

Contact a friend or mentor you trust and ask for honest feedback on one area you'd like to improve. Be specific in your request, and listen openly, without defensiveness. Take note of their insights and consider one change you can make based on their feedback. Embrace this as a step toward becoming your best self.

TODAY'S AFFIRMATION

I welcome honest feedback as a tool for growth and self-improvement.

JAN

FEB

MAR

APR

MAY

JUN

JUL

AUG

SEP

OCT

NOV

DEC

September 28

GROW WITH GRATITUDE

"Let us be grateful to the people who make us happy; they are the charming gardeners who make our souls blossom."

—MARCEL PROUST

Appreciation is the key to abundance. Every time you express gratitude, you plant a seed that allows more of that goodness to grow. When you take a moment to acknowledge the small, thoughtful gestures of others, you deepen your relationship with them and create a positive feedback loop. Gratitude is love in action. It uplifts others and brightens your day, filling it with more positivity.

TODAY'S ACTION

Be generous with your appreciation today. Notice the little things that bring you joy and acknowledge them out loud or with a kind gesture. Thank your barista for their cheerful smile, appreciate a coworker's helpfulness, or savor the warmth of your morning tea or coffee. Make it your mission to see and celebrate all the things, big or small, that make your day brighter. Allow yourself to grow in gratitude.

TODAY'S AFFIRMATION

The more I express gratitude, the more joy and abundance flow into my life.

September 29

NOURISH WITH POSITIVITY

"Don't let your mind bully your body."

—Astrid Alauda

Empowering your thoughts can empower your body.
Our mindset around food profoundly influences how
we feel about ourselves and our choices. When you
approach food with kindness and gratitude, you create
a nourishing relationship that uplifts your well-being.
Positive affirmations help with this. They are more than
words—they remind you of your commitment to a
healthy life. As you honor your body with affirmations, you
cultivate a loving, supportive connection with food.

TODAY'S ACTION

Write down three affirmations that resonate with you,
such as: "I nourish my body with love and positivity,"
"Each healthy choice fuels my energy," or "I trust my
body's needs." Place them on your fridge, desk, or phone,
and repeat them aloud whenever you see them. Notice
how this mindful approach to food uplifts your mood and
reinforces healthy choices.

TODAY'S AFFIRMATION

I nourish my body with love and positivity every day.

JAN
FEB
MAR
APR
MAY
JUN
JUL
AUG
SEP
OCT
NOV
DEC

September 30

CHOOSE YOUR HAPPINESS

"Saying yes to happiness means learning to say no
to things and people that stress you out."

—THEMA DAVIS

**Happiness is saying no to what drains you and yes to
what fills you.** It's a choice. Choosing happiness means
creating space for what brings you joy and peace. It's an
act of self-respect, a commitment to your well-being,
and a reminder that your joy matters. When you prioritize
happiness, you take ownership of your life and let go of
what no longer serves you.

TODAY'S ACTION

Set aside time to watch your favorite movie today. Share
the experience with someone special to double the joy.
Allow yourself to get lost in the story, feel each emotion,
and notice new details. Relish in the happiness that
comes from revisiting something you love.

TODAY'S AFFIRMATION

I embrace what brings me joy and allow happiness to fill
my life.

October

October 1

FOCUS IS KING

"Your life is controlled by what you focus on."

—Tony Robbins

What you focus on grows. Your attention shapes your experience, setting the tone for how you feel, act, and live. You empower yourself when you focus on goals, gratitude, and growth. By directing your energy toward the positive, you gain control over your life and align with what lights you up. Every moment is a choice to focus on positivity.

TODAY'S ACTION

Today, practice intentional focus. Choose one area where you want to see growth and positive change. Spend a few moments visualizing what success in this area looks like, and write down one small step you can take today to move closer to it. By focusing on what matters, you create a powerful path forward.

TODAY'S AFFIRMATION

I focus on what uplifts me and guides me toward my best life.

October 2

BE GENTLE WITH YOURSELF

"Do the best you can until you know better.
Then when you know better, do better."

—MAYA ANGELOU

You are doing your best, even if it doesn't always feel like it. Life has seasons; sometimes, the most powerful thing you can do is be gentle with yourself. Self-care is more than pampering. It's about treating yourself with the compassion you would offer a friend. When you give yourself grace, you make room to grow, heal, and become stronger. Remember, progress isn't always about giant leaps. It's about the small, gentle steps you take each day.

TODAY'S ACTION

Take a few moments today to do something kind for yourself. It could be as simple as a few deep breaths, a short walk outside, or a few quiet minutes with a good book or music. Reflect on what you need most, and give yourself permission to rest and recharge. Remind yourself that taking time for self-care isn't selfish—it's essential.

TODAY'S AFFIRMATION

I am gentle with myself, allowing space for rest and growth.

October 3

CHOOSE COMPASSION OVER JUDGMENT

"When you judge another, you do not define them, you define yourself."

—WAYNE DYER

Judging others reveals more about our hearts than theirs. Each time we choose compassion over judgment, we open ourselves to a deeper understanding. A compassionate heart sees others with grace instead of criticism. By guiding ourselves toward empathy, we let go of judgment and embrace the beauty of seeing others through a loving lens.

TODAY'S ACTION

Take a moment today to reflect on someone you've judged recently. Set an intention to replace judgment with compassion. Visualize seeing this person through a lens of understanding, and notice how this shift softens your perspective and guides your interactions. Compassion allows us to be more loving in our relationships.

TODAY'S AFFIRMATION

I let compassion guide my thoughts and actions every day.

JAN
FEB
MAR
APR
MAY
JUN
JUL
AUG
SEP
OCT
NOV
DEC

October 4

STAND UP TO OBSTACLES

"Stand up to your obstacles and do something about them. You will find that they haven't half the strength you think they have."

—NORMAN VINCENT PEALE

Optimism is the foundation of progress. When you face obstacles head-on, they often prove less daunting than they appeared. Challenges lose their power the moment you decide to act. Move forward with courage and a belief in your strength. Trust that within you is everything you need to overcome and grow stronger. When you bring optimism to your challenges, you transform setbacks into stepping stones.

TODAY'S ACTION

Identify one challenge you've been avoiding. Take a small step today to confront it, whether by making a plan, asking for advice, or tackling it directly. Notice how taking action can shift your perspective and empower you, even in small ways.

TODAY'S AFFIRMATION

I face my obstacles with optimism, knowing I can overcome them.

October 5

PROTECT YOUR PEACE

"Your peace is more important than driving yourself crazy trying to understand why something happened the way it did. Let it go."

—MANDY HALE

Peace comes when we release the need to understand everything. Life will always have moments that don't make sense, and holding on too tightly can drain our energy and joy. True peace is found in letting go and trusting that some things don't need our overthinking or endless analysis. When we let go, we make space for calm, clarity, and renewed well-being.

TODAY'S ACTION

Create a "Peace Place" in your home today. Find a quiet corner to retreat for moments of stillness and reflection. Bring in a cozy chair, blanket, or anything that brings comfort. Commit to spending a few minutes here each day this week, allowing yourself to be present and release any worries or need for control. Let this space be a daily reminder to choose peace over stress.

TODAY'S AFFIRMATION

I let go of what I cannot control and protect my peace.

JAN

FEB

MAR

APR

MAY

JUN

JUL

AUG

SEP

OCT

NOV

DEC

October 6

BUILD BETTER HABITS

"Motivation is garbage. It's never there when you need it. If you want to change your life, you have to change your choices and your habits."

—MEL ROBBINS

Your daily choices reveal what you truly value. How you spend your time speaks volumes about your priorities and self-worth. We unintentionally fill our most energized hours with tasks that don't align with our goals or values. By consciously evaluating your day's structure, you create space to honor your needs, focus on growth, and cultivate self-worth. Let today be an exercise in observing whether your routine is moving you toward the life you want—or holding you back.

TODAY'S ACTION

Look at how you spend your mornings when your energy and focus are highest. List your morning activities, then ask yourself: Are these actions aligned with my goals and well-being? Choose one activity supporting your growth and make it your priority tomorrow. Small changes can make a significant impact when they're rooted in purpose.

TODAY'S AFFIRMATION

I choose to build better habits that honor my priorities.

October 7

BUILD UNSHAKEABLE FAITH

"Faith activates God—fear activates the enemy."

—Joel Osteen

Faith is a powerful force that invites God's presence and guidance into your life. When you pray, you're not just speaking words but actively choosing faith over fear, trusting that God hears you and will respond. In times of uncertainty or challenge, prayer becomes your connection to divine strength and peace. With each prayer, your faith deepens, reminding you that no matter the circumstances, God is in control.

TODAY'S ACTION

Create a "Faith Journal" today to build unshakable faith. Set aside a notebook where you can write down your prayers and reflect on the ones answered over time. Begin by writing a prayer focused on an area where you seek to strengthen your faith. Revisit this journal over the days and weeks to record how God works in your life. This practice enriches your prayer life and allows you to see the blessings unfolding, big and small.

TODAY'S AFFIRMATION

I choose faith over fear, building a foundation of unshakeable trust.

October 8

OWN YOUR WELL-BEING

"You have the power to heal your life. We think so often that we are helpless, but we're not. We always have the power of our minds..."

—Louise Hay

Healing is a choice, and it starts with you. Every small, intentional action you take contributes to your overall well-being. Whether it's how you care for your body, the words you speak to yourself, or the habits you build, your daily choices nurture or neglect your health. Self-care is more than a luxury—it's a responsibility and a way of actively supporting your healing.

TODAY'S ACTION

Create your own Self-Care Jar with your family or just for yourself. Fill it with simple, uplifting activities that support your physical, mental, emotional, and spiritual health. Whenever you need a boost, pick a slip from the jar and let it remind you to take care of yourself. For daily self-care accountability, join the free challenge at 7daysofselfcare.com and make positivity a habit.

TODAY'S AFFIRMATION

I embrace my power to heal and care for myself every day.

JAN
FEB
MAR
APR
MAY
JUN
JUL
AUG
SEP
OCT
NOV
DEC

October 9

LEAD BY LEARNING

"The ability to learn is the most important quality a leader can have."

—SIMON SINEK

Learning is a superpower. It opens doors, sparks curiosity, and builds resilience. Each time you learn something new, you enhance your mind, boost your confidence, and expand your world. Authentic leaders embrace learning as a lifelong journey, knowing that every skill or insight brings them closer to their best selves.

TODAY'S ACTION

Choose one skill or topic you've been curious about. Dedicate just five or ten minutes today—and each day this month—to explore it. Watch how small steps add to real progress, whether it's a language, hobby, or personal interest. Start today, and by the end of the month, you'll see just how much you've grown!

TODAY'S AFFIRMATION

I am constantly growing and learning.

JAN
FEB
MAR
APR
MAY
JUN
JUL
AUG
SEP
OCT
NOV
DEC

October 10

IGNITE YOUR CREATIVE SPARK

"Creativity is intelligence having fun."

—ALBERT EINSTEIN

Creativity shines brightest when you're having fun. It's your secret superpower, bringing life to ideas and turning ordinary moments into inspiration. Einstein reminds us that the best ideas often come when we let go and enjoy the process. That's the power of play. When you infuse your day with creative play, joy meets inspiration, and possibilities are endless.

TODAY'S ACTION

Try something fun and creative new—doodle a quick sketch, write a short poem, or create a vision board. Set a timer for 10 minutes and dive in without overthinking. Afterward, reflect on how this burst of creativity energized you and opened new perspectives. Let this playful spark fuel the rest of your day!

TODAY'S AFFIRMATION

I embrace creativity with joy, letting inspiration flow freely.

October 11

GUIDED BY FAITH

"The moment you surrender to love and allow it to lead you to exactly where your soul wants to go, you will have no difficulty."

—NEALE DONALD WALSCH

Surrender is not about giving up. It's about letting go with trust. When you surrender to love, you invite divine guidance into your life. It's about releasing control and allowing a force greater than yourself to lead the way. True surrender opens the path to ease, grace, and the unfolding of something far more significant than you could have planned. Trust that you are being guided to exactly where you're meant to be.

TODAY'S ACTION

Take the "Faith Challenge". Identify an area in your life where you've been holding on tightly or trying to control the outcome. Take a deep, centering breath, and commit to surrendering this area to God. Consciously release it, saying a prayer of trust and asking for guidance and strength. Each time doubt or control creeps back in, remind yourself of this surrender, trusting that faith will lead you forward.

TODAY'S AFFIRMATION

I surrender with faith, knowing I am constantly being guided.

October 12

STAND IN YOUR POWER

"Stand tall, chin up, shoulders back—your
body language shapes who you are."

—AMY CUDDY

Your body speaks volumes. A power pose isn't just a
stance. It's a signal to yourself and the world. When you
stand tall, you tell your brain you're strong, capable, and
ready. This pose exudes confidence, sets boundaries, and
reflects a person with purpose. No wonder superheroes
stand this way—it's the posture of power.

TODAY'S ACTION

Start your day by holding this power pose for one minute.
Stand tall, hands on your hips, chin up, and chest open.
Add a subtle smile. Throughout the day, try this pose
before stepping into new situations—before errands,
meetings, conversations, or even sending an email.
Notice how this simple shift affects how you feel and how
others respond to you.

TODAY'S AFFIRMATION

I embody confidence, strength, and purpose.

October 13

TUNE IN TO YOUR BODY

"Most people have no idea how good their body is designed to feel."

—KEVIN TRUDEAU

Your body is a gift designed to support you in ways you might not even realize. Every breath, every step, and every heartbeat is a reminder of its incredible ability. When you honor and care for your body, you unlock its true potential. Studies show that nurturing this connection boosts immunity, lowers stress, and elevates mood. Feeling amazing isn't a luxury; it's your body's natural state. Respect your body. Appreciate it. Let it thrive.

TODAY'S ACTION

Practice body gratitude today. Stand in front of a mirror and thank your body for all it does. Acknowledge its strength, resilience, and support. Take it deeper by writing a thank-you note to your body, listing what you appreciate most. Let this act of body gratitude remind you to care for your body with kindness daily.

TODAY'S AFFIRMATION

I honor my body with gratitude and care, appreciating all it does for me.

October 14

TAKE BACK YOUR POWER

"Self-care is how you take your power back."

—Lalah Delia

Self-care is more than a break—it's an act of strength.
When you care for yourself, you reclaim your energy,
protect your peace, and honor your worth. Science
shows that self-care reduces stress, enhances emotional
resilience, and strengthens your immune system. Deep
self-care restores you and reminds you of your resilience.
In these moments, you reconnect with yourself and what
you need to feel whole and empowered.

TODAY'S ACTION

Engage in an act of deep self-care today. It could be
journaling to clear your mind, setting a boundary to
protect your energy, or recharging in nature. Choose
something that nourishes you and allows you to feel
renewed and grounded.

TODAY'S AFFIRMATION

I honor my power by choosing self-care and protecting
my well-being.

October 15

KEEP GOING AGAINST THE ODDS

"If something is important enough, you do it even if the odds are not in your favor."

—ELON MUSK

When something truly matters, the obstacles fade in importance. Real purpose doesn't wait for perfect conditions—it pushes forward despite them. Genuine commitment means stepping up, even when the path feels uncertain. By focusing on what you care about most, you draw on a strength that helps you rise above challenges, no matter the odds.

TODAY'S ACTION

Identify one crucial goal or passion you've set aside due to challenges or doubts. Take one small action today to move it forward, even if it's just a single step. Remember, commitment to what truly matters is more powerful than any obstacle in your way. You can do this!

TODAY'S AFFIRMATION

I am committed to what matters, moving forward with purpose and resilience.

JAN
FEB
MAR
APR
MAY
JUN
JUL
AUG
SEP
OCT
NOV
DEC

October 16

THE POWER OF SOLITUDE

"I think it's very healthy to spend time alone. You need to know how to be alone and not be defined by another person."

—Oscar Wilde

Solitude is essential for self-discovery. In the quiet of alone time, you reconnect with who you truly are beyond the expectations and influences of others. Being comfortable alone builds confidence, self-awareness, and inner strength. Time spent in solitude is time invested in knowing yourself more deeply—your thoughts, feelings, and desires.

TODAY'S ACTION

Dedicate a portion of the next 24 hours to disconnecting from distractions. Turn off your phone, step away from screens, and find a quiet space to be alone. Use this time to sit in stillness, walk in nature, or let your mind wander. Embrace the solitude, allowing yourself to reflect and recharge without the influence of external noise. If it's helpful, write in a journal afterward to document your insights and reflections.

TODAY'S AFFIRMATION

I cherish time alone as a chance to reconnect with my true self.

October 17

HONOR YOUR BODY'S WISDOM

"Your body is always talking to you. The question is: Are you listening?"

—Dr. Mindy Pelz

Your body speaks in whispers, guiding you toward balance and health. Through subtle signals and sensations, it tells you what it needs. Listening to your body means tuning into its wisdom and trusting it to lead you toward well-being. Paying attention, you unlock a deeper understanding of yourself, creating space for proper self-care.

TODAY'S ACTION

Take a few minutes to check in with your body. Close your eyes and scan from head to toe, noticing any tension, discomfort, or areas that feel good. Ask yourself what your body needs today—maybe a stretch, a glass of water, or some quiet time. Commit to honoring its request, knowing that even small acts of self-care can profoundly impact your well-being.

TODAY'S AFFIRMATION

I listen to my body and honor its needs with care and respect.

INSTANT POSITIVITY **315**

JAN
FEB
MAR
APR
MAY
JUN
JUL
AUG
SEP
OCT
NOV
DEC

October 18

PROGRESS OVER PERFECTION

"The decent method you follow is better
than the perfect method you quit."

—TIM FERRISS

Progress comes from consistency. A simple approach
you stick with will consistently outperform the flawless
routine that's impossible to maintain. Every small action
becomes a building block toward your goals when done
consistently. Remember, it's not about doing everything
perfectly—it's about showing up and taking steady steps
forward.

TODAY'S ACTION

Identify one simple, manageable health habit you
can stick with this week. It could be drinking a glass of
water first thing in the morning, adding an extra serving
of veggies to your meals, or doing a quick 10-minute
workout. Commit to it for seven days and focus on
building consistency over perfection.

TODAY'S AFFIRMATION

I make progress by taking small, consistent steps
every day.

October 19

MAKE IT PLAYFUL

"We don't stop playing because we grow old;
we grow old because we stop playing."

—George Bernard Shaw

Playfulness is the spark that keeps life fresh and joyful.
When we add a touch of fun to our daily routine, even
the simplest tasks can feel exciting. Play awakens our
creativity, lowers stress, and brings us fully into the
present moment. Playfulness is a gift we leave behind
as we grow older, yet it holds the power to refresh our
spirit and renew our perspective. Play can make even
the simplest routines feel lighter, reminding us that life is
meant to be enjoyed, not managed.

TODAY'S ACTION

Add a little fun to your routine! Skip to the kitchen, turn
your to-do list into a game, or reward yourself with
points for every arduous task you complete. Notice how
lighthearted moments can transform your day and boost
your energy.

TODAY'S AFFIRMATION

I infuse my day with joy and playfulness.

JAN

FEB

MAR

APR

MAY

JUN

JUL

AUG

SEP

OCT

NOV

DEC

October 20

WALK WITH PATIENCE AND FAITH

"Adopt the pace of nature: her secret is patience."

—Ralph Waldo Emerson

Nature reminds us that patience is its own kind of strength. The natural world unfolds without rush, trusting that every season has its purpose. When we connect with nature's steady rhythms, we must release our need for control and trust the process. Patience lets us find peace in life's timing, knowing everything blooms at the right moment.

TODAY'S ACTION

Take a walk in nature today—whether it's a park, a trail, or even your backyard. As you walk, focus on the world around you. Notice the small details: the rustling leaves, the steady flow of water, or the song of birds. Reflect on how nature's rhythms mirror the patience and trust required in your journey. Let this walk ground you in the calm assurance that your path will unfold in its own time, like nature.

TODAY'S AFFIRMATION

I walk in patience and faith, trusting life's natural rhythms to guide me.

October 21

WELCOME LIFE'S SURPRISES

"Life can still be beautiful, meaningful, fun, and fulfilling even if things don't turn out the way you planned."

—LORI DESCHENE

Life's beauty often lies in the unexpected. When we let go of expectations, we open ourselves to experiences that can surprise, teach, and lead us somewhere better. Embracing the unplanned moments invites growth. Trust that life is unfolding perfectly for you, and remember this: the best moments happen unexpectedly. Letting go of control creates space for magic, opportunity, and positivity.

TODAY'S ACTION

Reflect on when things didn't go as planned but led to a positive outcome or valuable lesson. Write down what you learned from that experience and how it contributed to your growth. As you go through your day, practice releasing minor frustrations or unmet expectations and look instead for the beauty and meaning in the unexpected.

TODAY'S AFFIRMATION

I trust life to surprise me with beautiful and meaningful experiences.

JAN

FEB

MAR

APR

MAY

JUN

JUL

AUG

SEP

OCT

NOV

DEC

October 22

HONOR YOUR BODY

"Take care of your body. It's the only place you have to live."

—Jim Rohn

Your body is your home and your most loyal companion. It's been with you through every challenge, supporting you daily. But how do you take a moment to acknowledge all it does for you? Your body works tirelessly, from your legs that carry you to your lungs that sustain you. It deserves your appreciation and care, even when it feels less than perfect.

TODAY'S ACTION

Today, take a moment to express gratitude to your body. Start your day by writing a simple thank-you note to yourself. Consider how your body has been there for you, from helping you complete daily tasks to giving you strength when needed. You can also show appreciation by doing something kind for your body today—enjoying a balanced meal, taking a short walk, going to the gym, or resting.

TODAY'S AFFIRMATION

I love and appreciate my body for all it does.

October 23

POWER IS IN FOCUS

"You can do anything, but not everything."

—David Allen

Trying to do it all dilutes your power. Progress comes from focus—choosing what matters most and letting go of the rest. When you prioritize with intention, you bring impact to everything you do. Remember, doing less allows you to give more to what truly matters, fueling your growth and joy.

TODAY'S ACTION

Create a "Focus List" for the day. Write down three things that truly matter to you—these are tasks or goals that align with your values, purpose, and positivity. As you go through the day, give your total energy to each item. Challenge yourself to let go of anything that doesn't support these priorities. By focusing intensely, you're building the habit of intentional progress and letting go of what doesn't serve your growth.

TODAY'S AFFIRMATION

I prioritize what truly matters, allowing my energy to fuel purposeful progress.

JAN

FEB

MAR

APR

MAY

JUN

JUL

AUG

SEP

OCT

NOV

DEC

October 24

FREEDOM IN FORGIVENESS

"Forgiveness frees your heart from the weight of others' actions."

—KRISTEN BUTLER

Forgiveness is a gift you give yourself. When you choose to forgive, you let go of the burden of others' actions on your heart. Forgiveness doesn't mean excusing what happened. It doesn't mean it's okay. It means you free yourself from the emotional chains that keep you stuck. You reclaim your peace and open space for healing and positivity by letting go. Remember, forgiveness is about releasing the weight—not for them, but for you.

TODAY'S ACTION

Identify someone or a situation that has been weighing on your heart. Please take a moment to breathe deeply and visualize releasing the hurt and resentment tied to it. Write a note to yourself or in your journal, expressing why you're choosing to forgive. Let this be a reminder that forgiveness is a powerful act of self-care, allowing you to move forward with a lighter heart.

TODAY'S AFFIRMATION

I release the weight of the past and embrace the freedom of forgiveness.

October 25

CALM AMONG CHAOS

"Calmness among chaos is a sign of emotional maturity."

—VEX KING

True calm isn't about avoiding chaos but staying grounded through it. Emotional maturity means finding your center, even when life feels overwhelming. Calmness is a choice—a sign of resilience and strength. When you can stay calm, you gain control and make better decisions. Calm is the foundation of emotional health and a powerful shield against burnout.

TODAY'S ACTION

Take a moment to check in with yourself. Are you feeling overwhelmed, exhausted, or stressed? These could be signs of burnout. Write down three things you can do this week to ease stress and recharge. Whether taking breaks, practicing mindfulness, spending time in nature, or simplifying your schedule, commit to protecting your well-being.

TODAY'S AFFIRMATION

I choose calmness and prioritize my well-being, allowing myself to recharge fully.

JAN

FEB

MAR

APR

MAY

JUN

JUL

AUG

SEP

OCT

NOV

DEC

October 26

ROUTINE AND REST RECHARGE

"Mornings belong to whatever is new; the current composition. Afternoons are for naps and letters."

—STEPHEN KING

There's a quiet magic in pausing in the middle of the day. While the morning brings fresh energy, the afternoon invites rest—a moment to breathe, reset, and refuel. This pause is a gift we give ourselves. When we allow space for rest, we invite calm, clarity, and strength into our lives. A simple nap can be a powerful act of renewal, aligning us with our best selves.

TODAY'S ACTION

Make the most of your morning, and then in the afternoon, find a quiet, comfortable spot and nap. Set an alarm so you can relax fully without worrying about time. Aim for a nap between 10 and 30 minutes—even if you rest without fully sleeping, you're gifting yourself a mental and physical recharge. If you're also looking for an empowering morning routine, download our free guide at riseandshineon.com.

TODAY'S AFFIRMATION

I honor the power of routine and rest to recharge my spirit.

October 27

LOVE WHAT YOU DO

"The only way to do great work is to love what you do."

—SIMON SINEK

Passion is the spark behind true greatness. When you love what you do, even the simplest tasks have meaning. It's not about just getting through the day. It's about pouring your heart into every action, big or small. Loving your work fuels creativity, resilience, and excellence. It's the love for what you do that turns challenges into opportunities. Embrace your work enthusiastically today, and watch how it elevates everything you touch.

TODAY'S ACTION

Choose one task you usually find routine or mundane, like answering emails, tidying your workspace, or working on a project. Add a twist that makes it enjoyable: play upbeat music, set a timer to challenge yourself, or reward yourself when you're done. Bringing a sense of play and purpose will reignite excitement and remind you why you love what you do.

TODAY'S AFFIRMATION

I bring passion and enthusiasm to everything I do.

JAN
FEB
MAR
APR
MAY
JUN
JUL
AUG
SEP
OCT
NOV
DEC

October 28

PROGRESS IN SMALL STEPS

"Your life will never improve unless you
start making daily improvements."

—Lewis Howes

Lasting change is built one small step at a time.
Significant transformations don't happen overnight—
they result from small, consistent actions that add up.
Today's quote reminds us that every tiny improvement is
a foundation for more significant growth. Each day, you
have the chance to make progress. When you commit
to steady, manageable steps, you create a path toward
meaningful, lasting change.

TODAY'S ACTION

Write a "1% Better" plan. Take one area of your life you
want to improve and break it down into a clear, step-
by-step roadmap. Define the most minor, specific
improvement you can make each day for the next
week—dedicating 5 minutes to meditation, practicing
a gratitude exercise, or setting a timer to read just one
page of a book. Write one sentence at the end of each
day about how this small action made you feel or
shifted your mindset. These small steps will deepen your
commitment to growth.

TODAY'S AFFIRMATION

I embrace daily progress, knowing small steps lead to
significant changes.

October 29

THE RIPPLE EFFECT OF POSITIVITY

"Positivity is contagious. Pass it on, and watch it grow."

—Kristen Butler

Every positive action creates a ripple that touches lives far beyond what you can see. A kind word, a simple smile, or a moment of encouragement can change someone's day—and maybe even their life. Positivity has a compounding effect, spreading light wherever it goes. Imagine the world you can help create by starting just one ripple. It begins with you.

TODAY'S ACTION

Be intentional about creating a 'Positivity Ripple Effect' today. Choose one act of kindness—a heartfelt compliment, a thoughtful message, or a small gesture of generosity. Reflect on how this action lifts your spirit and spreads positivity to others. Notice how the energy you create carries forward in unexpected ways.

TODAY'S AFFIRMATION

I am a source of positivity, and my actions create ripples of light and love.

JAN

FEB

MAR

APR

MAY

JUN

JUL

AUG

SEP

OCT

NOV

DEC

October 30

UNLOCK YOUR INFINITE POTENTIAL

"The power of imagination makes us infinite."

—John Muir

Imagination opens the door to limitless possibilities.
Your mind is powerful. Expanding our imagination, we
tap into potential far beyond our current limitations.
Through imagination, you can see pathways you didn't
know existed and allow your vision to lead you toward
something more significant. Trust in your dreams—they
are the seeds of your best life.

TODAY'S ACTION

Spend time today visualizing the best version of yourself.
Close your eyes and imagine life when fully aligned with
your true potential. If you're unsure, think of a problem
that moves you deeply, and consider how you might
help change it. Picture yourself as the person who
would fulfill this destiny—what qualities, achievements,
and experiences would you embody? Write down what
you see and reflect on how you can start taking small,
aligned actions each day to bring this vision to life.

TODAY'S AFFIRMATION

I trust in my limitless potential and believe in the power of
my dreams.

October 31

BELIEVE AND BECOME

"Whatever the mind can conceive and believe, it can achieve."

—Napoleon Hill

The power to create starts in the mind. When you believe in your vision, you activate the energy to bring it to life. Anything is possible when faith and imagination come together. Living your vision is about embodying the qualities, mindset, and actions of the person you want to become. When you genuinely believe in your dreams, you step into alignment, allowing flow to move you forward with ease.

TODAY'S ACTION

Identify one small, specific action you can take today that brings you 1% closer to your vision. It could be reading a chapter of a motivational book, making a meaningful connection, going longer at the gym, or dedicating ten extra minutes to a critical task. Commit to that step today, knowing that small, consistent actions are the building blocks of enormous success.

TODAY'S AFFIRMATION

I embody my vision confidently.

November

November 1

DREAM WITH BELIEF

"The future belongs to those who believe
in the beauty of their dreams."

—ELEANOR ROOSEVELT

Your dreams are the seeds of your future. When you
believe in them, you give them the power to grow. Belief
is the fuel that brings dreams to life. Trust in the beauty
of your vision, believe in its possibilities, and let it inspire
you to move forward. Every step you take, guided by faith,
shapes your desired future.

TODAY'S ACTION

Set aside 5-10 minutes to visualize your dream life as
if it's already yours. Close your eyes and dive into the
details—see, feel, and let it come alive. Write down one
clear action your future self would take today to live
that dream. Then, take that step right now. By aligning
with your vision, you bring it closer with each choice you
make. Let today be a turning point where your belief
transforms into action.

TODAY'S AFFIRMATION

I trust in the beauty of my dreams and take steps every
day to bring them to life.

JAN

FEB

MAR

APR

MAY

JUN

JUL

AUG

SEP

OCT

NOV

DEC

November 2

RELEASE YOUR OLD SELF

"Envisioning the end is enough to put the means in motion."

—Dorothea Brande

Creating the future starts with releasing the past. When we see our goals, we naturally begin moving toward them. Holding onto outdated beliefs or habits keeps us stuck in old versions of ourselves. Studies show that visualizing our goals can activate the subconscious mind to align with our desires. Letting go of what no longer serves us opens new growth and possibilities.

TODAY'S ACTION

Identify one old habit or belief that's holding you back. Please write it down and make a firm decision to release it today. Then, replace it with an empowering action—reframing a negative thought, starting a new routine, or embracing a mindset that supports your goals. You're choosing to step forward and become 1% better today by consciously letting go.

TODAY'S AFFIRMATION

I release the old and embrace the new, aligning my actions with my vision.

November 3

WRITE TO YOUR FUTURE SELF

"The more intensely we feel about an idea or a goal, the more assuredly the idea, buried deep in our subconscious, will direct us along the path to its fulfillment."

—EARL NIGHTINGALE

Emotions are the fuel for your dreams. Neuroscience shows that vividly imagining and emotionally connecting with our goals activates the brain's reward and motivation centers, which can increase our drive to achieve them. When you emotionally connect with your vision, you engage your subconscious to help shape your future. Let this connection inspire you to embrace what's possible.

TODAY'S ACTION

Write a letter to your future self dated one year from today. Describe your life as if all your dreams have already come true. Be specific about how you feel, what you've achieved, and who you've become. Infuse the letter with positive energy that goes beyond your current reality. You've got this!

TODAY'S AFFIRMATION

I connect deeply with my goals, trusting they guide me to fulfillment.

November 4

LIGHT UP YOUR SOUL

"The most powerful weapon on earth is the human soul on fire."

—FERDINAND FOCH

It's time to stand in your power. When you connect with your inner fire, you become unstoppable. True power isn't just physical—it's mental, emotional, and spiritual. Embracing your strengths and aligning with your purpose fuels your journey and lights the way forward. When you fully own who you are and what you stand for, you create a force that can overcome any obstacle.

TODAY'S ACTION

Write a "Power Statement" for yourself. Think of one area where you've held back, then write a bold declaration of what you're ready to embody moving forward. For example: "I am courageous in speaking my truth" or "I embrace my worth in all relationships." Say this statement out loud to yourself in the mirror, looking yourself in the eyes as you repeat it three times. Keep this statement close throughout the day, letting it remind you to step fully into your power.

TODAY'S AFFIRMATION

I stand in my power and let my inner fire guide me to greatness.

November 5

CONFIDENCE IN CONNECTIONS

"Confidence is not 'they will like me.'
Confidence is 'I'll be fine if they don't.'"

—SIMONE HENG

Absolute confidence is built on self-assurance rather than approval. It's knowing that others' opinions don't define your worth. Confidence is rooted in an unshakable sense of self. True power lies in your ability to be at peace with who you are, regardless of outside validation. You create an inner circle that fuels your self-worth by strengthening connections that uplift you and releasing those that drain you.

TODAY'S ACTION

Reflect on your closest relationships. Identify one relationship that consistently uplifts you and one that may hold you back. For the positive connection, find a meaningful way to nurture it—reach out, express gratitude, or plan a moment together. For the relationship that drains you, set a clear boundary or step back to protect your energy and confidence.

TODAY'S AFFIRMATION

I am confident in who I am, supported by connections that lift me higher.

JAN

FEB

MAR

APR

MAY

JUN

JUL

AUG

SEP

OCT

NOV

DEC

November 6

AWAKEN YOUR INNER STRENGTH

"You never know how strong you are until being strong is your only choice."

—BOB MARLEY

True strength is often revealed in life's most challenging moments. It's not always about pushing through with force; sometimes, quiet resilience helps you rise above. Your inner strength is a deep reserve, a constant reminder that you can handle whatever comes your way! When you connect with this strength, you discover a calm confidence that no obstacle can shake.

TODAY'S ACTION

Think back to a time when you showed resilience, even if it felt difficult. Write down three qualities you demonstrated during that experience. Let these qualities remind you of the strength already within you. Carry them with you today, trusting you're equipped for any challenge.

TODAY'S AFFIRMATION

My inner strength allows me to handle whatever comes my way.

November 7

BE PRESENT, BE POWERFUL

"You can't change the past, and you can't predict the future,
but you can choose to embrace the present moment."

—KRISTEN BUTLER

The present moment is where our power lies. In a world
that pulls us in many directions, it's easy to rush through
life on autopilot, always thinking about what's next. But
slowing down, even briefly, brings you back to what truly
matters. Research shows mindfulness improves focus
and productivity, reduces stress, and boosts well-being.
By being present, you give yourself the gift of peace,
clarity, and a chance to savor the positivity around you.

TODAY'S ACTION

Slow down and stay present with one task today. Savor
the moment. Whether making your morning lemon
water or coffee, writing an email, or taking a walk, do it
mindfully. Focus entirely on all the details—the smell, the
sounds, the sensations. Notice how this simple act can
change your whole mood!

TODAY'S AFFIRMATION

I find strength, peace, and positivity in the present
moment.

JAN
FEB
MAR
APR
MAY
JUN
JUL
AUG
SEP
OCT
NOV
DEC

November 8

ALIGN YOUR ATTITUDE

"Your attitude determines your altitude. Choose positivity, resilience, and gratitude, and watch how high you soar."

—David Meltzer

Your attitude is your power. It's the silent force behind every experience, shaping how far you'll go and how high you'll rise. Today's quote reminds us that a positive attitude is more than a mindset—it's the foundation for a fulfilling life. Each day, you can align with positivity, resilience, and gratitude. The right attitude will lift you above challenges and set the stage for growth. Let your attitude be the wind that carries you to new heights.

TODAY'S ACTION

Start your day by consciously choosing to elevate your attitude. Pick a straightforward action that reinforces this attitude—jotting down three things you're grateful for, sharing a kind word, or tackling a task enthusiastically. Throughout the day, whenever a challenge arises, pause and realign your response. Let every action align with positivity.

TODAY'S AFFIRMATION

I align my attitude with positivity, resilience, and gratitude, soaring to new heights.

November 9

NOURISH YOUR BODY

"When diet is wrong, medicine is of no use.
When diet is correct, medicine is of no need."

—AYURVEDIC PROVERB

What you eat fuels your body, mind, and spirit. This proverb reminds us that a healthy diet is the foundation of true wellness. Food is powerful. It can support your body's natural functions and help you thrive. Nourishing your body with the right foods is a way to care for your health from the inside out. When you eat mindfully, you give your body what it needs to stay vibrant and strong.

TODAY'S ACTION

Support your liver today by incorporating liver-friendly foods into your meals. Add leafy greens, beets, garlic, turmeric, cruciferous vegetables (like broccoli and Brussels sprouts), citrus fruits, and walnuts. Drink plenty of water to keep your liver hydrated and functioning at its best. Reflect on how these conscious choices help your body function more efficiently and impact your well-being.

TODAY'S AFFIRMATION

I nourish my body with mindful choices that support my health and vitality.

November 10

CULTIVATE ABUNDANCE

"Empty pockets never held anyone back.
Only empty heads and empty hearts can do that."

—Norman Vincent Peale

A wealthy mindset sees opportunities where others see limitations. Wealth starts within. It's not about the money in your pocket but the attitude you bring to life. It's driven by creativity, resilience, and a heart full of purpose. True abundance begins with a positive, empowered outlook that opens doors, fuels growth, and attracts success. When your mind is focused on abundance, your actions will naturally follow.

TODAY'S ACTION

Take one clear, practical step to strengthen your financial foundation. Set up an automatic transfer to your savings, review and adjust any unnecessary expenses, or research a new investment opportunity. Let this step be a small but powerful commitment to your financial future. With consistency, these actions create a ripple effect toward financial freedom and abundance.

TODAY'S AFFIRMATION

Money flows to me quickly and easily.

November 11

CREATE YOUR WINNING FORMULA

"It's your responsibility to find your winning formula."

—CLIONA O'HARA

Success isn't one-size-fits-all—it's personal. Your path is unique and shaped by your choices, strengths, and lessons. Creating a winning formula means owning your journey, learning what works best for you, and aligning with the habits that elevate you. It's about embracing your power to design a life that feels fulfilling to you. When you take charge of your success, you create a roadmap that leads you exactly where you're meant to go.

TODAY'S ACTION

This year is a story of your growth. Take time to reflect. What were your biggest wins? What were the lessons that shaped you most? Write down three strategies that helped you succeed and three areas to improve. Use these insights to craft your "winning formula" for the upcoming year, setting the stage for even more significant growth.

TODAY'S AFFIRMATION

I honor my journey and create a winning formula for my success.

JAN

FEB

MAR

APR

MAY

JUN

JUL

AUG

SEP

OCT

NOV

DEC

November 12

FOCUS ON THE GOOD

"No matter what's happening, choose to be happy. Don't focus on what's wrong. Find something positive in your life."

—JOEL OSTEEN

Happiness is a choice—a decision you make moment by moment. Life may bring challenges, but where you place your focus shapes your experience. Even in tough times, there's always something good to see, something worth celebrating. When you focus on the positive, you open your life to more joy and gratitude. It's about finding the silver linings, savoring small joys, and recognizing the beauty in each day.

TODAY'S ACTION

Pause and identify one positive thing in your life right now. Whether it's a simple pleasure like a warm cup of coffee, a kind word from a friend, or a beautiful view, please take a moment to feel gratitude for it. Savor it. Please write it down and let this small reminder bring peace and appreciation to your day.

TODAY'S AFFIRMATION

I focus on the good, choosing joy and gratitude in each moment.

November 13

LEAVE A LASTING IMPRESSION

"Dress shabbily and they remember the dress; dress impeccably and they remember the woman."

—Coco Chanel

How you dress speaks volumes before you say a word.
Dressing with intention is a powerful way to command respect and embrace your worth. Every detail in your appearance tells a story, showcasing your confidence, care, and self-respect. Let your style reflect the best of who you are. Step out as the most empowered version of yourself as often as possible, and you'll always leave a lasting impression.

TODAY'S ACTION

Choose an outfit that feels like the best version of yourself, no matter the occasion. Let it reflect who you are becoming. Whether at work, running errands, or spending time with loved ones, dress with intention. Notice the energy shift, the uplifted confidence, and how you feel seen. Dressing with purpose can be transformative—let it elevate your day.

TODAY'S AFFIRMATION

I carry myself with purpose, letting my style reflect my inner strength.

FEB

MAR

APR

MAY

JUN

JUL

AUG

SEP

OCT

NOV

DEC

November 14

LET YOUR SMILE SHINE

"Every time you smile at someone, it is an action of love, a gift to that person, a beautiful thing."

—Mother Teresa

A smile is an instant connection. It's a spark of kindness, a light that lifts the room. When you smile, you remind others they're seen. It's a silent gift that speaks volumes. Today, let your smile be your gift to others. Think of it as your superpower, creating positivity wherever you go.

TODAY'S ACTION

Smile at five people today—whether friends, family, or strangers. Feel the shift in your mood. Feel the change in their mood and the lightness it brings. Notice how one small act can change everything around you. Allow the power of your smile to open hearts and create memorable moments.

TODAY'S AFFIRMATION

My smile radiates warmth and creates positivity wherever I go.

November 15

SHAPE TOMORROW TODAY

"You cannot escape the responsibility of
tomorrow by evading it today."

—ABRAHAM LINCOLN

Today's actions are the seeds of tomorrow's success.
Every step is an investment in your desired future, no
matter how small. Dreams don't simply happen; they're
built through consistent, intentional daily choices.
Committing to moving forward, even in the slightest
way, creates a ripple effect that brings your goals within
reach. This commitment isn't about perfection but steady
progress and showing up for yourself with purpose.

TODAY'S ACTION

Choose one tangible action that supports a meaningful
goal. It could be planning, reaching out for support, or
gaining knowledge in an area you want to grow. Please
write it down, prioritize it, and move forward confidently.
Each step builds momentum, making tomorrow's vision
more achievable.

TODAY'S AFFIRMATION

I shape my future by taking inspired action today.

November 16

ACT WITH COURAGE

"Courage is the most important of all the virtues because, without courage, you can't practice any other virtue consistently."

—Maya Angelou

Courage is the strength that grounds every other virtue.
It's the foundation that helps us live with purpose and integrity. Courage allows us to act on our beliefs, even when it is difficult. Acting with courage means trusting in your strength, pushing through fear, and standing firm in your faith. When you root your courage in faith, you're ready to face any challenge, knowing you're never alone.

TODAY'S ACTION

Identify a situation where you've felt hesitant to take action or held back. Today, take one bold step forward, no matter how small. Embrace the courage within you, trusting that it will guide you. This step, supported by faith, reminds you that you can overcome any obstacle.

TODAY'S AFFIRMATION

My courage is rooted in faith, empowering me to take bold steps forward.

November 17

PAUSE TO RESPOND

"Between stimulus and response, there is a space. In that space lies our power to choose our response. In our response lies our growth and our freedom."

—Viktor E. Frankl

There's incredible power in the pause. The space before your response is a gateway to growth, a chance to choose your actions with intention. In that brief time, you can rise above impulse and act from your present self. This is where actual freedom lives—the freedom to create a life shaped by your integrity and values, not impulsive reactions. Today, let the pause be your strength.

TODAY'S ACTION

The next time you feel triggered or pressured, take a deep breath and pause. Use this space to choose a response that reflects your values and who you are. Practicing this pause enhances emotional intelligence and empowers you to live with greater purpose and control.

TODAY'S AFFIRMATION

I embrace the power of the pause, choosing my responses with intention.

November 18

POSITIVELY AFFIRM WHAT YOU WANT

"The positive thinker sees the invisible, feels the intangible, and achieves the impossible."

—Winston Churchill

Positivity is a powerful tool for transformation. A positive mindset allows you to see beyond your current reality, feel the truth of your desires, and pursue what others may deem impossible. Positive affirmations are a way to train your mind to focus on what you want, not on what you fear. When you affirm your dreams, you set the stage for them to take shape. Studies show that self-affirmation can reduce stress and boost problem-solving by broadening your perspective and building resilience. Today, let your words pave the way for your dreams.

TODAY'S ACTION

Let's use affirmations to become 1% better today. Write down three affirmations that reflect your deepest desires. Repeat them throughout the day, especially during moments of doubt or negativity. By consistently affirming what you want, you strengthen your belief in achieving it, making the impossible possible.

TODAY'S AFFIRMATION

I affirm my desires with unwavering positivity, knowing I can achieve my dreams.

November 19

PAUSE TO FIND PEACE

"Meditation pauses the story in your mind long enough for you to remember that your mind is always telling you a story."

—CORY ALLEN

Meditation provides you with a moment of stillness.
It allows you to step back and observe the stories your mind creates. By pausing, you give yourself the space to find clarity and peace, which can help you better navigate life's challenges. Research shows regular meditation can reduce stress, increase emotional resilience, and improve overall well-being. It acts as a reset button for your mind, helping you break free from the cycle of overthinking and anxiety. Today, let meditation be your anchor to find calm and clarity within.

TODAY'S ACTION

Take five minutes to sit quietly and focus on your breath. Close your eyes, take a deep breath, and let the tension in your body melt away. Notice when your mind starts to wander and gently guide it back to your breath. Even a few minutes of meditation can help lower stress and bring a sense of calm. Remember, each return to the breath is a step toward peace.

TODAY'S AFFIRMATION

I take time for stillness and connect with the deep peace within me.

JAN

FEB

MAR

APR

MAY

JUN

JUL

AUG

SEP

OCT

NOV

DEC

November 20

RISE ABOVE SETBACKS

"Failure at some point in your life is inevitable,
but giving up is unforgivable."

—JOE BIDEN

Failure is simply part of the journey. Everyone faces setbacks, challenges, and moments when things don't go as planned. However, failure does not define us; the resilience and courage we show when getting back up is what truly matters. Each stumble becomes an opportunity to learn, adjust, and grow stronger. By choosing not to give up, you turn every setback into a stepping stone toward success, embodying the power of perseverance.

TODAY'S ACTION

Think of a recent setback or challenge you've faced. Reflect on what it taught you and how to carry it forward. Write down one small, positive step you can take today to move closer to your goal, no matter how small. Every step you take is a choice to keep going, bringing you closer to the life you envision.

TODAY'S AFFIRMATION

I rise above setbacks and embrace each challenge with resilience.

November 21

CREATE SPACE FOR ABUNDANCE

"For every minute spent organizing, an hour is earned."

—Benjamin Franklin

Clearing clutter opens up space for clarity, abundance, and flow. When we take time to organize, we create room for what truly matters, letting go of what's weighing us down. Even a tiny step can symbolize a fresh start, making each item purposeful. Imagine each minute spent on this task as an investment into your peace of mind and a more intentional, abundant life.

TODAY'S ACTION

Today take a few minutes to clear and organize your purse or wallet. Lay out each item and ask yourself if it truly belongs there. Remove old receipts, expired cards, or anything that no longer serves you. If you find unused gift cards, plan to treat yourself soon! Consider this a small yet powerful step toward a life filled with intention and purpose. Notice how light and energized you feel as you let go of what you don't need.

TODAY'S AFFIRMATION

As I clear away clutter, I welcome clarity and abundance into my life.

JAN

FEB

MAR

APR

MAY

JUN

JUL

AUG

SEP

OCT

NOV

DEC

November 22

RESTORE YOUR SPIRIT IN NATURE

"There is no better way to calm your mind, recharge your soul, and awaken your inner wisdom than to spend time in nature."

—Brené Brown

Nature is the ultimate healer of the mind, body, and soul. Being in nature isn't just relaxing—it's proven to aid well-being. Studies show that time in natural environments can lower stress, lift your mood, and even strengthen your immune system. The sights, sounds, and scents of the outdoors invigorate your senses, grounding you in the present. No matter where you are, nature gives you a deep level of peace.

TODAY'S ACTION

Spend at least 10 minutes outside today. Take a walk, sit in a park, or step out for a breath of fresh air. Notice the details—the rustling leaves, the warmth of the sun, the coolness of the breeze. Let nature's calming presence restore your spirit and clear your mind.

TODAY'S AFFIRMATION

Nature nurtures my soul, bringing me peace, clarity, and renewal.

November 23

LET INTUITION BE YOUR FRIEND

"Intuition is the most honest friend that you will ever have."

—DOE ZANTAMATA

Your intuition often knows the path before your mind does. Intuition is more than just a feeling. It's a reliable guide. Spiritually connected to your creator, who acts as your inner wisdom. By trusting and following your intuition, you align with your true self and make decisions that honor your values and desires. Studies show that intuitive thinking can reduce anxiety and increase confidence, helping you face challenges calmly and confidently.

TODAY'S ACTION

Pay attention to your first instinct in a situation today. Instead of second-guessing or asking for a second option, trust that initial feeling. Then, take inspired action on it. Notice how your intuition offers valuable insights and leads to more authentic outcomes. Over time, you'll get more consistent with being decisive.

TODAY'S AFFIRMATION

I trust my intuition as a loyal friend, guiding me toward my best path.

JAN

FEB

MAR

APR

MAY

JUN

JUL

AUG

SEP

OCT

NOV

DEC

November 24

CLEAR THE CLUTTER WITHIN

"Tidying is the act of confronting yourself."

—MARIE KONDO

Letting is about discovering what truly belongs in your life. It's a chance to see yourself with clarity. Each item we hold onto reflects a part of us, whether it's a memory, a habit, or a feeling we haven't let go of. Tidying gives us a moment to pause and decide what we want. By intentionally choosing what to keep and what to release, we create space for what matters, both in our surroundings and hearts.

TODAY'S ACTION

Set aside a few minutes to tackle a closet or junk drawer. Take each item out and decide if it's useful or meaningful. Keep what serves you, and let go of the rest. Use dividers or small containers to keep items organized and accessible. As you put everything back, notice how light and empowered you feel. Clearing even a tiny space can create clarity and calm throughout your day.

TODAY'S AFFIRMATION

I create space for what truly matters in my life.

November 25

POSITIVITY FUELS PROGRESS

"Challenges can't stop you. People can't stop you. Time can't stop you. Your negative thoughts can. Stay positive."

—KRISTEN BUTLER

Positivity is your secret strength. Challenges and setbacks will always arise, but your mindset determines your path. Shifting your perspective empowers you to see obstacles as opportunities and embrace growth. When you choose positivity, you unlock the resilience and courage needed to move forward.

TODAY'S ACTION

Take charge of your thoughts today. Whenever you notice a negative thought, pause and actively reframe it. For example, if you're facing a challenging task or feeling doubtful, remind yourself of your inner strength and look for a positive angle. Watch how this simple shift uplifts your outlook and energizes your day.

TODAY'S AFFIRMATION

I am stronger than any challenge, and my positivity fuels my progress.

JAN

FEB

MAR

APR

MAY

JUN

JUL

AUG

SEP

OCT

NOV

DEC

November 26

PRAY, BELIEVE, AND RECEIVE

"Therefore I tell you, whatever you ask in prayer, believe
that you have received it, and it will be yours."

—MARK 11:24

Faith turns hope into certainty. Faith is more than hope.
The unwavering belief that what you ask for in prayer
is already done. This powerful verse reminds us that
belief is the key that opens us to receive the blessings
we seek. When you pray, hold your vision close, trust
in God's perfect timing, and know His promises are
already in motion. This faith transforms your prayers into
affirmations of what's possible and invites blessings into
your life.

TODAY'S ACTION

Take a moment to visualize a goal or dream you've been
praying for. Write it down in a journal, and beside it, write,
"I believe it is already done." Throughout your day, carry
this belief, trusting that God is working behind the scenes
to support you in every step.

TODAY'S AFFIRMATION

I believe in God's timing and receive His blessings with
gratitude.

November 27

HONOR YOUR RESILIENCE

"You are stronger than you think, braver than you believe, and smarter than you know."

—A.A. MILNE

What you focus on grows. Recognizing and appreciating your strengths builds a solid foundation of confidence and reinforces a positive self-image. How often do you honor your unique abilities? Identifying your skills reminds you of your power, helping you face challenges and quickly seize new opportunities.

TODAY'S ACTION

Write a list of your top skills. Reflect on the abilities that make you shine and how they've contributed to your successes. Take a moment to appreciate each one, and let this recognition fill you with confidence and excitement for the future. You are stronger, braver, and smarter than you give yourself credit for.

TODAY'S AFFIRMATION

I honor and celebrate my strengths and talents.

JAN

FEB

MAR

APR

MAY

JUN

JUL

AUG

SEP

OCT

NOV

DEC

November 28

THE POWER OF FLOWERS

"Flowers always make people better, happier, and more helpful; they are sunshine, food, and medicine to the soul."

—LUTHER BURBANK

Flowers have a unique ability to lift our spirits and our spaces. Their vibrant colors, delicate shapes, and gentle fragrances remind us of the beauty and positivity around us. When we bring flowers into our home, we invite a bit of nature's magic into our daily lives. Creating a bouquet can be deeply soothing, bringing joy, creativity, and a sense of calm.

TODAY'S ACTION

Treat yourself to a bouquet of fresh flowers today. Take time to choose and arrange them in a joyful and fulfilling way. Consider making this a family activity if you have children—let them pick a flower to add to the arrangement. Let the beauty and fragrance of the flowers serve as a reminder to appreciate life's little gifts.

TODAY'S AFFIRMATION

I welcome beauty and joy into my life each day.

November 29

LOVE YOURSELF UNCONDITIONALLY

"Self-love has very little to do with how you feel about your outer self. It's about accepting all of yourself."

—Tyra Banks

True, unconditional love comes from embracing who you are, inside and out. When you can love yourself well, you can love others deeply. It's about honoring every part of yourself beyond appearances. When you accept all of who you are, you feel seen and valued from within, allowing you to reflect that same love to others.

TODAY'S ACTION

Stand in front of the mirror and give yourself three genuine compliments. Focus on qualities, actions, or strengths you appreciate about yourself. Let each compliment sink in. Feel the warmth and positivity it brings. Notice how this simple act strengthens your self-worth. Self-compliments aren't just lovely—they're essential. They remind you of your worth and build confidence that no one can shake.

TODAY'S AFFIRMATION

I love, honor, and appreciate my unique qualities.

JAN

FEB

MAR

APR

MAY

JUN

JUL

AUG

SEP

OCT

NOV

DEC

November 30

GROWTH IS THE KEY TO SUCCESS

"Your success is inevitable when you're willing to work on yourself."

—Evan Carmichael

Success begins with a commitment to growth. This kind of commitment isn't about quick wins. It's about the daily decision to become your best self. When you're willing to work on yourself, you open the door to boundless possibilities. Each small step forward is a testament to your resilience. Each goal achieved brings you closer to the success of your future self.

TODAY'S ACTION

Choose one habit or skill you'd like to develop further. Write a brief plan outlining how you'll work on this area daily, even in small ways. Commit to this process for the next 30 days. You have one more month left in this year. Make it one you are proud of. Keep a journal to reflect on your progress. Notice how small actions compound over time and build your confidence.

TODAY'S AFFIRMATION

I am dedicated to my growth, knowing that each step leads me toward my success.

December

CHOOSE GOOD CHEER

"Even in a strange and difficult year, the
Bible says, 'Be of good cheer.'"

—BILLY GRAHAM

Positivity means finding light, even within challenges.
When you embrace a spirit of cheer, you lift your heart
and inspire others. Research shows that maintaining
a positive outlook in difficult times can reduce stress,
improve health, and increase resilience. By consciously
choosing good cheer, you remind yourself there's always
hope, no matter the circumstances.

TODAY'S ACTION

Take a "Cheer Check" every few hours today. Pause,
smile, and think of one thing you're grateful for, even if
it's small. Let this moment of cheer reset your mood and
bring peace. Over time, these small acts of gratitude
and joy can become a powerful habit that transforms
your day.

TODAY'S AFFIRMATION

I choose to be of good cheer, bringing light to every
moment.

JAN
FEB
MAR
APR
MAY
JUN
JUL
AUG
SEP
OCT
NOV
DEC

December 2

HONOR YOUR NEEDS

"You don't have to struggle in silence. You can be un-silent."

—DEMI LOVATO

You don't have to carry everything on your own. When you speak your needs, you honor your worth and open the door to support and understanding. In a world that often rewards quiet endurance, choosing to be "un-silent" is an act of strength. Expressing what you need creates space for deeper connections and reminds you that your well-being matters. Your voice is powerful. Use it to create the life you deserve.

TODAY'S ACTION

Reflect on an area where your needs aren't met. Choose someone you trust and share your needs openly, with honesty and courage. Release any self-judgment and focus on creating a genuine connection. When you advocate for yourself, you invite others to stand by you, strengthening your resilience and relationships.

TODAY'S AFFIRMATION

I honor my needs and welcome support into my life.

December 3

EMBRACE YOUR INNER BEST FRIEND

"The challenge is… learning to be my own best friend instead of my own worst critic."

—KRISTEN BUTLER

We're harder on ourselves than anyone else ever could be. Our inner dialogue can be overly critical, focusing on flaws instead of strengths. But what if you could see yourself through the eyes of someone who loves you? A best friend doesn't fixate on your imperfections. They see your unique qualities, kindness, and all the little things that make you extraordinary. Embracing that perspective can open the door to greater self-compassion and self-love.

TODAY'S ACTION

Imagine your best friend is sitting across from you. Ask yourself, "How would they describe me?" Better yet, call them and ask! Write down or record their words to revisit them whenever you need a reminder of your worth. Let their words sink in, and allow yourself to feel loved and appreciated. Then, take a moment to return the favor and share what you love most about them.

TODAY'S AFFIRMATION

I see myself through a lens of kindness and love.

JAN

FEB

MAR

APR

MAY

JUN

JUL

AUG

SEP

OCT

NOV

DEC

December 4

LOOK UP AT THE STARS

"Be glad of life because it gives you the chance to love,
to work, to play, and to look up at the stars."

—Henry Van Dyke

The expansion of the Universe has a way of grounding us. When we look up at the stars, we're reminded of how connected we are to the beauty of creation. Gazing at the night sky invites a quiet sense of awe, helping us release daily worries and feel a peaceful presence beyond ourselves. It's a simple way to pause, reflect, and let go.

TODAY'S ACTION

Step outside for a few moments tonight and look up at the sky, gazing at the stars if it's clear enough. Breathe in the fresh air, wrap yourself in the quiet of the night, and feel the vastness of the Universe. As you look up, let your mind relax and your heart open to the beauty and mystery of creation. Notice how your worries fade as you reconnect with this sense of wonder and expansion.

TODAY'S AFFIRMATION

I breathe in peace and feel connected to the Universe.

December 5

FOCUS ON THE PRESENT

"The power for creating a better future is contained in the present moment: You create a good future by creating a good present."

—ECKHART TOLLE

Presence is the ultimate experience of this reality. Your worries fade when you tap into the present moment and lose track of time. You become fully alive. This state of flow is deeply satisfying, bringing a sense of balance and positivity. By immersing yourself in the present, you create a life filled with purpose and connection.

TODAY'S ACTION

Schedule a "Flow Hour" today to dive into an activity you enjoy and find slightly challenging. Choose something that excites you. Silence notifications, set a one-hour timer, and immerse yourself completely, letting go of any need for perfection. Afterward, reflect on how you felt during this focused time—notice any increased sense of calm, joy, or clarity. Consider making this Flow Hour a regular ritual to stay connected to the present and recharge.

TODAY'S AFFIRMATION

As I focus on the present moment, I enter the perfect flow of life.

JAN

FEB

MAR

APR

MAY

JUN

JUL

AUG

SEP

OCT

NOV

DEC

December 6

JOY IS WITHIN US

"Joy is not in things; it is in us."

—Richard Wagner

Positivity is in the little joys of daily life. Recognizing and appreciating these small moments fills your day with a steady stream of positive energy. Each time you savor a small pleasure, like a warm cup of coffee, a kind word, or a quiet moment, you create space for gratitude and contentment within you. Happiness grows not by chasing it but by noticing it in the everyday.

TODAY'S ACTION

Today, make it a point to notice three small moments that bring you joy. It could be anything—a comforting routine, a smile from a friend, or a favorite song. Pause and appreciate these moments fully. Feel the joy they bring within you, and let that positivity carry you through your day.

TODAY'S AFFIRMATION

I find joy in the simple moments, filling my day with positivity and gratitude.

December 7

LIVE WITH PURPOSE

"Living with intention brings value to your life."

—Lauren Magers

Living intentionally means choosing actions that align with who you are and what you truly want. When you're clear on your purpose, each decision becomes an opportunity to add meaning to your day. From the relationships you nurture, the children you raise, and the friends you make to the goals you pursue, intentional choices create a purpose-filled life. You don't have to wait for big moments either; your small, deliberate daily actions bring you closer to a life aligned with your values and desires.

TODAY'S ACTION

Reflect on one area of your life where you could bring more intention. Consider what small change would make it feel more purposeful, whether it's a habit, a relationship, or a daily routine. You can even journal about it if you feel inspired. Then, take one step today toward aligning yourself with this desire.

TODAY'S AFFIRMATION

I live with purpose, bringing intention and meaning to each day.

December 8

LET GO OF PERFECTION

"Perfection is not attainable, but if we chase perfection we can catch excellence."

—Vince Lombardi

Letting go of perfection frees you to grow and learn with ease. Striving for perfection can create unnecessary pressure, but focusing on excellence allows room for mistakes and progress. When you shift your mindset from perfect to purposeful, you open yourself to new possibilities. Embrace your journey and imperfections, and recognize that your best effort is enough. True success comes from progress, not perfection.

TODAY'S ACTION

Reflect on an area where you may be holding onto perfection. Consider one small change you can make to release this pressure. Instead of doing it perfectly, focus on it with energy and intention. Take one step forward with this new perspective.

TODAY'S AFFIRMATION

I release the need for perfection and embrace growth in every step.

JAN
FEB
MAR
APR
MAY
JUN
JUL
AUG
SEP
OCT
NOV
DEC

December 9

STEP BEYOND YOUR LIMITS

"Most great people have attained their greatest success just one step beyond their greatest failure."

—NAPOLEON HILL

Success often arrives right after moments of challenge. When you feel you're on the edge of what's possible, that's usually the moment when a breakthrough is within reach. Each setback and failure is part of the journey, helping you clarify your intentions and redefine your goals. Greatness lies in being willing to take another step and set new intentions that move you forward with resilience and positivity.

TODAY'S ACTION

Reflect on a challenge you're currently facing and set a new intention that helps you move through it. For example, if you've been stuck on a project, intend to approach it with fresh ideas or seek support to help you progress. Write down this intention, and outline one small action step you'll take toward it today. Let this intention give you purpose, clarity, and a fresh perspective. When you set new intentions, you open yourself to growth and new possibilities.

TODAY'S AFFIRMATION

I set new intentions that help me step beyond limits and reach new heights.

JAN

FEB

MAR

APR

MAY

JUN

JUL

AUG

SEP

OCT

NOV

DEC

December 10

FREEDOM THROUGH FORGIVENESS

"Forgiveness is not an occasional act; it is a constant attitude."

—MARTIN LUTHER KING JR.

Forgiveness is a gift of freedom we give ourselves.
Resentment is a weight that drags us down, stealing our positivity. Holding onto it is like clutching a burning coal—only you get hurt. When we release resentment, we make space for healing. Forgiveness doesn't mean acceptance. It simply means choosing freedom over pain. This act of release allows us to step forward with a light heart and open to new possibilities.

TODAY'S ACTION

Today, take a moment to let go of one lingering resentment. Write down what you feel toward the person or situation, and then, as an act of release, tear up the paper or safely burn it. Visualize the weight lifting off your shoulders as you commit to letting go. Shift your focus toward something you're grateful for, allowing that positive energy to fill the space where resentment once lived.

TODAY'S AFFIRMATION

I let go of resentment and welcome peace into my heart.

December 11

LOVE YOUR REFLECTION

"Success is liking yourself, liking what you
do, and liking how you do it."

—Maya Angelou

**Loving yourself begins with accepting the person you
see in the mirror.** True confidence comes when you
accept how you naturally look, radiating authenticity
in the world. This level of self-love isn't about meeting
society's beauty standards—it's about recognizing and
celebrating what makes you uniquely you. Letting go of
the need to be "perfect" and appreciating your natural
beauty nurtures a sense of self-worth that shines from
the inside out.

TODAY'S ACTION

Look in the mirror today with fresh eyes. Smile at yourself,
offer a compliment, and view your reflection with
kindness. Notice what you love about your face—the little
quirks, the smile lines, the sparkle in your eyes. Release
self-criticism and see yourself with the warmth and
acceptance you'd give to someone you love.

TODAY'S AFFIRMATION

I am beautiful, inside and out.

JAN

FEB

MAR

APR

MAY

JUN

JUL

AUG

SEP

OCT

NOV

DEC

December 12

SET CLEAR GOALS

"Setting goals is the first step in turning
the invisible into the visible."

—TONY ROBBINS

Goals transform ideas into action. Without a clear goal,
you're like a driver without a destination, circling without
progress. Goals bring purpose, guiding your energy and
focus toward a specific outcome. When you set concrete
goals, you target your mind and heart, aligning your daily
actions with the future you're creating.

TODAY'S ACTION

Begin today by setting three clear goals for yourself—
personal, professional, or simply about self-care. Write
them down to give them weight. Keep these goals in
mind as you go through the day, letting them guide
your choices. Tonight, reflect on your progress and set
three new goals for tomorrow. Each small win builds your
momentum.

TODAY'S AFFIRMATION

I turn my dreams into reality by setting clear, achievable
goals.

December 13

PLAY TO WIN

"When you play, you play to win. You don't do it by half measures."

—ELON MUSK

When you set your mind to something, go all in. Half-hearted effort only leads to half-hearted results. Playing to win isn't just about achieving the goal—it's about the commitment and passion you bring to each step. When you approach your dreams with full energy and dedication, you set yourself up for success, knowing you gave it everything you had.

TODAY'S ACTION

Identify one goal or task you've been approaching with hesitation or a half-hearted effort. Decide to commit to it today and watch yourself soar fully. Eliminate distractions, focus on giving it your best, and exceed your usual expectations. Notice how it feels to pursue your goal with a "play to win" mentality.

TODAY'S AFFIRMATION

I bring my full energy and commitment to everything I do.

NOURISH WITH MINDFULNESS

"Mindful eating is a powerful practice that fosters a deeper connection with yourself and the world around you."

—Uma Naidoo, MD

Eating is more than fueling your body. It's an invitation to slow down, connect, and be present. Mindful eating is a way to honor your body and nourish your soul. Each bite is an act of self-care, a moment of gratitude, and a celebration of the nourishment your body deserves. When you eat mindfully, you cultivate a deeper appreciation for your body and well-being.

TODAY'S ACTION

Choose one meal today to practice mindful eating. Turn off distractions, take time with each bite, and focus on the flavors, textures, and aromas. Notice how your body feels as you eat, and stop when you feel satisfied, not stuffed. Reflect on how this practice deepens your relationship with food and brings a sense of gratitude.

TODAY'S AFFIRMATION

I eat mindfully, honoring my body and nourishing my soul.

December 15

FIND POSITIVITY IN NATURE

"Sunsets are proof that no matter what happens,
every day can end beautifully."

—KRISTEN BUTLER

When you need inspiration, look to nature. Watching the sunset is a simple yet impactful way of connecting with the world around you. The vibrant colors, quiet stillness, and gradual fading of light remind us of life's natural rhythms and the beauty of letting go. If you're feeling stressed, insecure, or doubtful, the sunset can gently remind you to pause, reset, and find your spark again.

TODAY'S ACTION

Travel to your favorite spot to watch the sunset today. As you take in the moment's beauty, reflect on what inspires you and consider how to bring that sense of wonder into your daily life. Allow yourself to be filled with calmness and possibility. When you appreciate the natural miracle of a sunset, you invite peace and gratitude into your life.

TODAY'S AFFIRMATION

I find inspiration and peace in nature.

December 16

TAKE INSPIRED ACTION

"The universe rewards action. Take inspired action towards your goals, and miracles will unfold."

—David Meltzer

The path to abundance is paved with inspired action.
When you follow intuitive nudges and act on what feels right, you open the door to miracles. Inspired action is different from effort or force; it comes from a place of alignment and trust. This kind of action transforms visions into reality with ease and flow. Abundance isn't just about attracting things—it's about stepping into the rhythm of life, where life meets you halfway, unfolding blessings along the way.

TODAY'S ACTION

Take inspired action. Choose one goal you're passionate about and think of a small but meaningful action to move it forward. Take this action today, and as you do, believe each step aligns you closer to the abundance you seek. Trust that this one small action has the power to create momentum.

TODAY'S AFFIRMATION

I take inspired action, trusting that abundance and miracles are unfolding in my life.

JAN FEB MAR APR MAY JUN JUL AUG SEP OCT NOV DEC

December 17

LOVE UNCONDITIONALLY

"The best thing to hold onto in life is each other."

—AUDREY HEPBURN

Genuine connection is one of life's greatest gifts. Connecting with others through kindness and unconditional love creates bonds that make life abundant and more beautiful. Moments of thoughtfulness and care deepen these connections, bringing warmth and joy beyond the gesture.

TODAY'S ACTION

Plan a small, thoughtful surprise for someone who could use a bit of extra love today. Think of a friend, family member, or colleague, and choose a gesture to make them feel appreciated. Whether it's treating them to coffee, sending a heartfelt note, or offering a helping hand, tailor the surprise to reflect what would uplift them most. Enjoy the simple happiness that giving brings.

TODAY'S AFFIRMATION

I lift others with kindness, filling my heart with joy.

JAN
FEB
MAR
APR
MAY
JUN
JUL
AUG
SEP
OCT
NOV
DEC

December 18

EMBRACE YOUR FUTURE SELF

"Your future self is calling you to blaze the trail."

—Benjamin P. Hardy

Visualizing your future self is a powerful motivator for personal growth. You create a clear path toward that reality by aligning your current actions with the aspirations of who you want to become. The science behind this concept, known as 'future self-continuity,' shows that when you view your future self as a real, distinct individual, you're more likely to make choices that support long-term goals over immediate gratification. This mental connection helps create a clear roadmap to your desired future.

TODAY'S ACTION

Take a moment to vividly imagine your future self—consider your achievements, habits, and the life you lead. Write a letter from the perspective of this future self to your present self, offering guidance, encouragement, and insights. Reflect on the steps you can take today to align with this vision and commit to one actionable change that brings you closer to becoming that person.

TODAY'S AFFIRMATION

I am actively becoming the best version of myself.

December 19

CLARITY CREATES SUCCESS

"Your vision is a pathway to purpose."

—LISA GUILLOT

Clarity gives you power. When you have a clear vision, you're not wandering—you're moving with intention and purpose. A strong vision provides direction, fueling each step you take toward creating the life you truly want. As you enter a new year, aligning with your vision brings you closer to living a life that reflects your authentic self. Embrace the journey, knowing that clarity doesn't always come all at once but through each intentional step forward.

TODAY'S ACTION

Prepare for the new year by thinking about what you want to create. Reflect on one meaningful goal for each area of your life—health, relationships, career, and personal growth. Write down these goals and how they align with your vision. Use this exercise to fuel your intentions as you enter the new year, setting a foundation for purpose and fulfillment. If you feel stuck, check out the book *Find Your Clear Vision*.

TODAY'S AFFIRMATION

I am open to aligning with my vision and committed to bringing it to life.

JAN
FEB
MAR
APR
MAY
JUN
JUL
AUG
SEP
OCT
NOV
DEC

December 20

SHOW APPRECIATION FOR YOURSELF

"Everyone wants to be appreciated, so if you appreciate someone, don't keep it a secret."

—MARY KAY ASH

Your love for yourself fuels the love you give to others. It's hard to pour from an empty cup—when you're depleted, it's challenging to show up fully in your relationships. One way to replenish your energy is by appreciating yourself. Acts of self-love pay great dividends, positively impacting how you connect with others. When you recognize your worth and treat yourself with kindness and respect, you inspire others to treat you with the same love. Self-love radiates outward, enriching your relationships, boosting your confidence, and attracting more positivity.

TODAY'S ACTION

Reflect on something you've done recently that makes you proud. Please write it down and acknowledge your efforts and achievements. Speak to yourself as you would to someone you admire and love deeply. Acts of self-appreciation allow you to love yourself more fully, making it easier to receive love from others.

TODAY'S AFFIRMATION

I appreciate and love myself for who I am.

STAY STRONG IN STORMS

"You can't get to courage without walking through vulnerability."

—Brené Brown

Positivity isn't about ignoring challenges but finding strength within them. True resilience is born when we face our struggles with courage, knowing that each difficulty can teach us something valuable. Allowing ourselves to be vulnerable creates space for growth, self-compassion, and deeper connections. Positivity in tough times is a choice that empowers you to learn, adapt, and ultimately grow stronger.

TODAY'S ACTION

Create a "Strength in the Storms" list. Write down three challenging situations from your past where you found strength, resilience, or growth. Next to each situation, write a sentence about how that experience positively impacted who you are today. Reflect on this list whenever you face difficulties, reminding yourself that your inner strength comes from overcoming life's storms.

TODAY'S AFFIRMATION

I choose resilience and courage, knowing that every challenge helps me grow.

JAN

FEB

MAR

APR

MAY

JUN

JUL

AUG

SEP

OCT

NOV

DEC

December 22

IMPACT LEADS TO SUCCESS

"Success is not about how much money you make; it's about the difference you make in people's lives."

—Lewis Howes

True success grows from impact. When you focus on the positive difference you can make, success becomes more than just an achievement—it becomes a force for good. Learning from others who've reached their dreams reminds you that real success comes from serving, inspiring, and uplifting others. Each story of impact shows you that success is best when shared. The more lives you touch, the more abundant your journey becomes.

TODAY'S ACTION

Find a story that highlights impact, whether a biography, podcast, or article. As you listen or read, focus on how this person uplifted others to achieve success. Write down a powerful lesson from their journey and identify one action you can take today to make a positive difference in someone else's life. Let their story guide you in creating your impact.

TODAY'S AFFIRMATION

I create success by making a positive difference in the world.

December 23

USE GRATITUDE OVER WORRY

"Gratitude turns what we have into enough, transforming even the simplest moments into opportunities for joy and growth."

—Nick Hutchison

Gratitude is the antidote to uncertainty. In a stressful world, getting caught up in worries is easy. But gratitude can flip the script, turning anxiety into peace. Studies show that focusing on what you're thankful for can lower stress and bring more joy and clarity. When you appreciate what you have, even the smallest challenges can be an opportunity for growth.

TODAY'S ACTION

Instead of getting stuck in "what-if" worries, grab hold of "what-is" gratitude! Think of three things going right in your life—no matter how small. Is it the way your coffee tasted this morning? Or the fact that your favorite podcast has a new episode? Focus on those little wins, and let them shift your mindset to abundance and joy.

TODAY'S AFFIRMATION

I choose to see life through a grateful lens.

JAN
FEB
MAR
APR
MAY
JUN
JUL
AUG
SEP
OCT
NOV
DEC

December 24

FAITH IN THE UNSEEN

"With God all things are possible."

—MATTHEW 19:26

Faith opens the door to possibilities that go beyond our understanding. When you align with a higher power, you can overcome challenges with resilience and courage, knowing you are not alone. Believing means trusting that there's a way forward, even when things seem uncertain. This mindset allows you to see life with hope and strength. It will enable you to move confidently toward your dreams, knowing you're not alone.

TODAY'S ACTION

Think of an area where you've been feeling discouraged or losing hope. Take a few quiet moments to pray, asking for renewed strength, guidance, and the courage to keep going. Pray for the ability to see new possibilities and to trust that God is working behind the scenes. Close your prayer with gratitude, thanking God for the hope and support that sustain you. Let this prayer breathe life back into your heart and reignite your belief in what's possible.

TODAY'S AFFIRMATION

I trust in the power of faith, knowing that all things are possible with God.

LOVE ONE ANOTHER

"Love one another. As I have loved you,
so you must love one another."

—JOHN 13:34

Christmas is the reason for the season. The season
of love is a reminder to reach out with kindness and
compassion. Jesus' message calls us to embrace
each other wholeheartedly, as He loved us—freely and
unconditionally. This holiday, let's reflect on how we
can share that love with family and friends and all we
encounter. When we extend grace and kindness, we bring
the true spirit of Christmas into the world.

TODAY'S ACTION

Make a list of three simple ways you can show love to
others today—through a small act of kindness, a genuine
compliment, a gift, or reaching out to someone who may
need connection. Let each action remind you of the joy of
loving without limits because He first loved us.

TODAY'S AFFIRMATION

I choose to love others freely, with grace and
compassion.

JAN

FEB

MAR

APR

MAY

JUN

JUL

AUG

SEP

OCT

NOV

DEC

December 26

WORK SMARTER, LIVE FULLER

"Doing less is not being lazy. Don't give in to a culture that values personal sacrifice over personal productivity."

—TIM FERRISS

Busyness sometimes means progress. It's easy to confuse constant action with productivity in a world glorifying hustle. But the secret to a fuller life is learning to work smarter, not harder. When we focus on what truly matters, we free up time and energy for what we love. Simplifying your day, prioritizing high-impact tasks, and letting go of the rest can create the space to live more fully, with purpose and freedom.

TODAY'S ACTION

Identify one task you can streamline, delegate, or let go of today. Ask yourself, "Does this move me closer to my goals, or is it simply filling time?" Take one small step toward simplifying your workload—saying "no" to an extra commitment, automating a routine task, or setting aside focused time for a high-priority goal.

TODAY'S AFFIRMATION

I choose purpose over busyness and create space for what truly matters.

SHOW APPRECIATION FOR OTHERS

"Spread love everywhere you go. Let no one ever come to you without leaving happier."

—Mother Teresa

You have the power to make someone's day brighter by expressing appreciation. Letting the people you love know how much they mean to you is one of the most uplifting habits you can cultivate. We all want to feel seen, recognized, and valued. When you show appreciation, you create a more profound sense of connection and remind them—and yourself—of the abundance of love and support surrounding you. Your bonds with others are at the heart of a fulfilling life.

TODAY'S ACTION

Take a moment today to express genuine appreciation for someone you care about. Let them know what you value about them. Thank them for something specific they've done or a unique quality you cherish. Notice how this small act strengthens your bond and brings joy to both of your lives.

TODAY'S AFFIRMATION

I am grateful for the positive impact my loved ones have on my life.

December 28

REMEMBER THE GOOD

"Memories are perhaps the best gifts of all."

—GLORIA GAITHER

Memories are gifts that keep our hearts full and lift our spirits. When you focus on the good moments in life, you create a well of positivity that fuels your resilience and joy. Dwelling on the best parts of your past helps you move through life with a grateful heart, knowing there's always something worth remembering, even in tough times. Life is richer and more meaningful when you cherish what brings you joy and strength.

TODAY'S ACTION

Start a "Good Moments" journal today. Write down a positive memory from today or your recent past, describing what it meant to you and how it made you feel. By focusing on these moments, you'll make it a habit to see the good and add more positivity to your day.

TODAY'S AFFIRMATION

I choose to remember and celebrate the good in my life.

JAN
FEB
MAR
APR
MAY
JUN
JUL
AUG
SEP
OCT
NOV
DEC

COMBAT FEAR WITH GRATITUDE

"When you are grateful, fear disappears and abundance appears."

—Dr. Joe Vitale

Fear can be overwhelming. It can hold you back from pursuing your dreams, enjoying the present moment, and connecting deeply with those around you. When fear takes hold, seeing the possibilities and blessings surrounding you is hard. But gratitude is a powerful antidote. When you focus on what you're grateful for, you shift your perspective from scarcity to abundance. Gratitude grounds you in the present, reminding you of what is good and working in your life. It diminishes fear's power, opening the door to positivity and possibility.

TODAY'S ACTION

Today, whenever fear creeps in, pause and list three things you're grateful for. Allow feelings of appreciation to well up in your heart. This practice isn't about ignoring your fears but soothing and transforming them by acknowledging what's already good in your life. When you see the good, more good finds you.

TODAY'S AFFIRMATION

I combat fear with gratitude.

JAN

FEB

MAR

APR

MAY

JUN

JUL

AUG

SEP

OCT

NOV

DEC

December 30

SHARE YOUR HEART

"The more you love, the more love you have to give.
It's the only feeling we have which is infinite…"

—CHRISTINA WESTOVER

**Love is a boundless force, and the more we share it,
the more it grows.** Expressing love creates a positive
ripple effect, deepening connections and nourishing
the heart. Love isn't something we store up and keep to
ourselves; it's something we give freely, expanding as it's
shared. One of the most powerful ways to honor this is by
creating a "love list"—a collection of heartfelt reasons you
appreciate someone special.

TODAY'S ACTION

Today, create a "love list" for someone special. Write
down all the reasons you love and appreciate them.
If you feel comfortable, consider sharing the list with
them as a meaningful gesture. Even if you keep your
love list private, you'll still activate the energy of love
within yourself, bringing warmth and joy into all areas of
your life.

TODAY'S AFFIRMATION

My relationships are filled with love, gratitude, and deep
connection.

EMBRACE YOUR NEXT CHAPTER

"Write it on your heart that every day is the best day in the year."

—Ralph Waldo Emerson

The year is ending, but your journey is just beginning. Each day is a fresh page, inviting you to write your story with intention. Reflect on how far you've come—every challenge, victory, and quiet moment of growth has prepared you for this moment. Step into the new year with renewed purpose, knowing that the path to a positive life is in the small, daily steps. Every day has the potential to be your best day.

TODAY'S ACTION

Create a "Vision Time Capsule" for the year ahead. Write a letter to your future self, setting down your deepest intentions, dreams, and affirmations for the new year. Imagine a year from now, looking back on all you've accomplished and who you've become. Seal this letter and put it somewhere safe. Next New Year's Eve, open it and reflect on the powerful journey you visualized today.

TODAY'S AFFIRMATION

I am grateful for the past and embrace my future with confidence, courage, and joy.

Endnotes

Throughout this book, we've explored various aspects of positivity, personal growth, and well-being. Research from leading experts, spiritual texts, and influential books supports the shared insights and practices. Below are some of the key sources that informed this book's content:

American Heart Association. (2019). "Walking for Heart Health." Studies show that regular walking reduces the risk of heart disease, boosts mental clarity, lowers anxiety, and enhances overall mood by releasing endorphins and supporting brain health. https://www.heart.org/en/healthy-living/fitness/walking

American Heart Association. *The Benefits of Cardiovascular Exercise.* Available at: https://www.heart.org/en/healthy-living/fitness/fitness-basics/aha-recs-for-physical-activity-in-adults

American Journal of Public Health. (2005). "Benefits of Service: Providing Support Reduces Mortality." https://ajph.aphapublications.org/doi/abs/10.2105/AJPH.2005.064170

American Psychological Association. "Emotional Resilience and Positive Thinking." APA. https://www.apa.org/topics/resilience

American Psychological Association. (2012). "Mindfulness and Emotional Regulation." https://www.ncbi.nlm.nih.gov/pmc/articles/PMC3679190/

Bechara, A., Damasio, H., & Damasio, A. R. (2000). "Emotion, Decision Making, and the Orbitofrontal Cortex." Cerebral Cortex, 10(3), 295–307.

Beck, Judith S. *Cognitive Behavior Therapy: Basics and Beyond.* 3rd ed., Guilford Press, 2020.

Bratman, G. N., Hamilton, J. P., Hahn, K. S., Daily, G. C., & Gross, J. J. (2015). *Nature experience reduces rumination and subgenual prefrontal cortex activation.* Proceedings of the National Academy of Sciences, 112(28), 8567–8572. https://doi.org/10.1073/pnas.1510459112

Brown, Brené. *Atlas of the Heart: Mapping Meaningful Connection and the Language of Human Experience.* Random House, 2021.

Brown, Stuart L., and Christopher C. Vaughan. *Play: How It Shapes the Brain, Opens the Imagination, and Invigorates the Soul.* New York: Avery, 2009.

Carnegie Mellon University. (2018). "The Power of Self-Affirmation." https://www.cmu.edu/dietrich/news/news-stories/2018/August/self-affirmation.html

Chevalier, Gaétan, et al. "Earthing (grounding) the human body reduces blood viscosity—a major factor in cardiovascular disease." The Journal of Alternative and Complementary Medicine, vol. 19, no. 2, 2013, pp. 102–110.

Darby, Amy, and Catherine Harris. "Clutter, chaos, and the 'home as project': Managing and making sense of clutter in contemporary everyday life." Sociology of Health & Illness, vol. 40, no. 8, 2018, pp. 1452–1467.

Doidge, Norman. *The Brain That Changes Itself: Stories of Personal Triumph from the Frontiers of Brain Science.* Viking, 2007.

Emmons, Robert A., and Laura A. King. "Thematic analysis, meaning, and life satisfaction." Journal of Personality and Social Psychology, vol. 64, no. 6, 1993, pp. 1061–1072.

Emmons, R. A., & McCullough, M. E. (2003). "Counting blessings versus burdens: An experimental investigation of gratitude and subjective well-being in daily life." Journal of Personality and Social Psychology, 84(2), 377–389. https://pubmed.ncbi.nlm.nih.gov/12585811/

Ferriss, Tim. *The 4-Hour Workweek: Escape 9-5, Live Anywhere, and Join the New Rich.* Crown Publishing Group, 2007.

Ferriss, Tim. *The 4-Hour Body: An Uncommon Guide to Rapid Fat-Loss, Incredible Sex, and Becoming Superhuman.* Crown Archetype, 2010.

Fogg, B.J., *Tiny Habits: The Small Changes That Change Everything,* Houghton Mifflin Harcourt, 2019.

Fox, G. R., Kaplan, J., Damasio, H., & Damasio, A. (2015). "Neural correlates of gratitude." Frontiers in Psychology, 6, 1491.

Frankl, V. E. "Emotional Intelligence and Decision-Making." APA. https://www.frontiersin.org/articles/10.3389/fpsyg.2019.01768/full

Gigerenzer, G. (2007). *Gut Feelings: The Intelligence of the Unconscious*. Viking.

Goyal, Madhav, et al. *Meditation Programs for Psychological Stress and Well-being: A Systematic Review and Meta-analysis.* JAMA Internal Medicine, 2014.

Greater Good Science Center. (n.d.). "The Science of Gratitude." Greater Good Science Center, University of California, Berkeley. https://ggsc.berkeley.edu/images/uploads/GGSC-JTF_White_Paper-Gratitude-FINAL.pdf?_ga=2.51257770.246418475.1638563377-157927757.1638563377

Guillot, Lisa. *Find Your Clear Vision: A New Mindset to Create a Vibrant Personal or Professional Brand with Purpose.* Morgan James Publishing, 2022.

Hardy, Benjamin. *Be Your Future Self Now: The Science of Intentional Transformation.* Hay House, 2022.

Harvard Health Publishing. "Relaxation Techniques: Breath Control Helps Quell Errant Stress Response." Harvard Medical School. https://www.health.harvard.edu/mind-and-mood/relaxation-techniques-breath-control-helps-quell-errant-stress-response

Harvard Medical School. "Liver Health and Dietary Choices." https://www.ncbi.nlm.nih.gov/pmc/articles/PMC3942738/

Harvard Medical School. "Spirituality May Help People Live Longer." Harvard Medical School. https://www.health.harvard.edu/mind-and-mood/spirituality-may-help-people-live-longer

Harvard T.H. Chan School of Public Health. "Health Benefits of Regular Exercise." https://www.hsph.harvard.edu/news/hsph-in-the-news/health-benefits-regular-exercise-mental-health/

Harvard Medical School. *The Health Benefits of Walking.* Available at: https://www.health.harvard.edu/staying-healthy/5-surprising-benefits-of-walking

Harvard Health Publishing. "The Importance of Stretching." Harvard Health Publishing, May 2020.

Heinrichs, M., von Dawans, B., & Domes, G. (2009). "Oxytocin, vasopressin, and human social behavior." Frontiers in Neuroendocrinology, 30(4), 548-557. https://doi.org/10.1016/j.yfrne.2009.05.005

Hodgkinson, G. P., Langan-Fox, J., & Sadler-Smith, E. (2008). "Intuition in Decision-Making." British Journal of Psychology.

Howes, Lewis. *The Greatness Mindset: Unlock the Power of Your Mind and Live Your Best Life Today.* Hay House, 2023.

Journal of Social Cognitive and Affective Neuroscience. (2015). "Positive Affirmations and Self-Concept." https://academic.oup.com/scan/article/10/3/343/1680803

King, Vex. *Good Vibes, Good Life: How Self-Love is the Key to Unlocking Your Greatness.* Hay House, 2018.

Koch, S. C., Kunz, T., Lykou, S., & Cruz, R. (2014). "Effects of dance movement therapy and dance on health-related psychological outcomes." The Arts in Psychotherapy, 41(1), 46-64.

Kondo, Marie. *The Life-Changing Magic of Tidying Up: The Japanese Art of Decluttering and Organizing.* Ten Speed Press, 2014.

Malik, V. S., & Hu, F. B. (2015). "Fructose and Cardiometabolic Health: What the Evidence from Sugar-Sweetened Beverages Tells Us." The Journal of the American College of Cardiology, 66(14), 1615-1624.

Martin, Rod A. "Sense of humor and physical health: Theoretical issues, recent findings, and future directions." Humorvol. 14, no. 1, 2001, pp. 1-19.

Mayer, Emeran A. *The Mind-Gut Connection: How the Hidden Conversation Within Our Bodies Impacts Our Mood, Our Choices, and Our Overall Health.* Harper Wave, 2016.

Mayo Clinic, "Aromatherapy for Health and Wellness." updated August 2021. https://newsnetwork.mayoclinic.org/discussion/home-remedies-what-are-the-benefits-of-aromatherapy/

Mayo Clinic. "Laughter and Stress Reduction." https://www.mayoclinic.org/healthy-lifestyle/stress-management/in-depth/stress-relief/art-20044456

Mayo Clinic. "Power of Forgiveness." https://www.mayoclinic.org/healthy-lifestyle/adult-health/in-depth/forgiveness/art-20047692

Mayo Clinic. (n.d.). "Self-Care: Engage in regular self-care practices." Mayo Clinic. https://www.mayoclinic.org/healthy-lifestyle/stress-management/in-depth/self-care/art-20044157

McGill, Stuart M. *Low Back Disorders: Evidence-Based Prevention and Rehabilitation*. 2nd ed., Human Kinetics, 2007, pp. 113-120.

Miyazaki, Y., & Park, B.J. (2010). "The healing benefits of forests." Environmental Health and Preventive Medicine,15(1), 27–37.

National Center for Complementary and Integrative Health. (n.d.). "Meditation: In Depth." NCCIH. https://www.nccih.nih.gov/health/meditation-in-depth

National Institute for Play. "The Science of Play." NIFP. https://www.nifplay.org/what-is-play/the-science/

National Library of Medicine. (2019). "Mindful Eating and Body Awareness." https://www.ncbi.nlm.nih.gov/pmc/articles/PMC6623762/

Neff, K. D. (2003). "Self-compassion: An alternative conceptualization of a healthy attitude toward oneself." Self and Identity, 2(2), 85-101.

Neff, Kristin D. "The role of self-compassion in emotional resilience and well-being." Self and Identity, vol. 10, no. 3, 2011, pp. 278-290.

Oettingen, G., & Mayer, D. (2002). *The motivating function of thinking about the future: Expectations versus fantasies.*Journal of Personality and Social Psychology, 83(5), 1198-1212.

Peale, N. V. *The Power of Positive Thinking*. This book is foundational for concepts of faith, positivity, and resilience reflected in the affirmations and actions in *Instant Positivity*.

Pennebaker, James W., and Joshua M. Smyth. *Opening Up by Writing It Down: How Expressive Writing Improves Health and Eases Emotional Pain*. New York: The Guilford Press, 2016.

Popkin, B. M., D'Anci, K. E., & Rosenberg, I. H. (2010). *Water, hydration, and health. Nutrition Reviews,* 68(8), 439-458. This study discusses the essential role of water in physiological functions, including its impact on mood, energy, and cognitive function.

PubMed. (2013). "Intentional Reading and Mental well-being." https://pubmed.ncbi.nlm.nih.gov/24348366/

Qing Li. (2018). "Forest Bathing for Stress Reduction." International Journal of Environmental Research and Public Health. https://pubmed.ncbi.nlm.nih.gov/30091656/

Ratey, John J. *Spark: The Revolutionary New Science of Exercise and the Brain.* Little, Brown and Company, 2008.

Reisch, Walter. Quoted in *The Power of Rest: Why Sleep Alone is Not Enough*. Penguin, 2006.

ScienceDirect. (1999). "Smiling and Positive Social Interactions." https://www.sciencedirect.com/science/article/abs/pii/ S0005796799000925

Shah, Amy. *I'm So Effing Tired: A Proven Plan to Beat Burnout, Boost Your Energy, and Reclaim Your Life*. Houghton Mifflin Harcourt, 2021.

Shrier, Ian. "Does Stretching Improve Performance? A Systematic and Critical Review of the Literature." Clinical Journal of Sport Medicine, vol. 14, no. 5, 2004, pp. 267–273.

Sonnentag, S., & Fritz, C. (2007). "The Recovery Experience Questionnaire: Development and Validation of a Measure for Assessing Recuperation and Unwinding from Work." Journal of Occupational Health Psychology, 12(3), 204-221.

Te Morenga, L., Mallard, S., & Mann, J. (2013). "Dietary sugars and body weight: Systematic review and meta-analyses of randomized controlled trials and cohort studies." BMJ, 346, e7492.

The Holy Bible. New International Version. Zondervan, 2011. Offers timeless spiritual wisdom on gratitude, kindness, love, forgiveness, and faith, grounding many reflections in *Instant Positivity*.

Visualization Techniques and Goal Achievement. (2003). *Tandfonline*. https://www.tandfonline.com/doi/abs/10.1080/10413200305400

Williams, Florence. *The Nature Fix: Why Nature Makes Us Happier, Healthier, and More Creative*. W.W. Norton & Company, 2017.

Young, Simon N. "How to increase serotonin in the human brain without drugs." Journal of Psychiatry & Neuroscience, vol. 32, no. 6, 2007, pp. 394–399.

Zaccaro, A., et al. (2018). *How breath-control can change your life: A systematic review on psycho-physiological correlates of slow breathing. Frontiers in Human Neuroscience*, 12, 353.

SPREAD
A LITTLE
Positivity!

Thank you for being here and for choosing Instant Positivity. Your support means the world to me!

Let's create a ripple effect of kindness and help others who need this book find it.

Here are a few simple ways you can make a big impact:

- **SHARE THE JOY:** Gift a copy to a friend who could use a boost or send them a quick note to check it out.

- **SHOUT IT OUT:** Leave a review on Amazon, Goodreads, or your favorite book retailer. Your words can inspire someone to take that first positive step!

- **SNAP & SHARE:** Take a photo of your book and post it on social media. Tag me [@positivekristen] so I can celebrate with you. YAY!

Your time and support are truly appreciated.

Thank you

for spreading positivity—you're making a difference!

About the Author

Kristen Butler is a 3x bestselling author, CEO, and Founder of Power of Positivity, a global movement she built from the ground up, now with over 50 million followers and reaching millions worldwide. Recognized as SUCCESS Magazine's Emerging Entrepreneur, Kristen helps her community embrace positivity, self-worth, and personal transformation.

Kristen shares the practical, empowering strategies and mindset shifts that helped her rebuild her life after hitting rock bottom in 2009 through her books, transformative courses, and talks. Featured on *TODAY, Forbes, Entrepreneur,* and *CBS*, Kristen is also a Keynote Speaker in business and personal development.

LET'S STAY CONNECTED!

- 🌐 www.positivekristen.com
- **f** facebook.com/positivekristen
- 📷 instagram.com/positivekristen
- 𝕏 X.com/positivekristen

Made in the USA
Middletown, DE
29 December 2024

68448353R00225